AF729935

Advancing the Agency of the Child

Theological and Methodological Principles

Rohan P. Gideon

Christian World Imprints

© Rohan P. Gideon

First Published in 2024 by

Christian World Imprints
Christian Publishing & Books from India
A-71 Group, Wazirpur Industrial Area
Delhi-110052
cwidelhi2017@gmail.com
www.ChristianWorldImprints.com
Phone: +91 11 41526079

ISBN: 978-93-6065-847-2 (HB)
ISBN: 978-93-6065-002-5 (PB)

All rights are reserved. No part of this publication can be reproduced, distributed, performed, publicly displayed, stored in a retrieval system, made into a derivative work, transmitted or utilized in any form or by any means; electronic, mechanical, photocopying, recording or any information storage system, without the prior written permission of the copyright holder(s), as indicated, and the publishers.

Jurisdiction: Any conflict or dispute in relation to this publication shall be adjudged in accordance with the laws of India and the matter shall be subject to the jurisdiction of the Courts, Tribunals or any other Forums of New Delhi, India, only.

Disclaimer: The views, facts, contents, any copyright material used and analysis arrived at in this publication are solely of the Author(s) who assert/s the right to be identified as Author(s); the Publisher does not take any responsibility for the same in any manner whatsoever.

Printed in India.

Contents

Acknowledgements

"Language exists less to record the actual than to liberate the imagination." These words of the English writer and composer Anthony Burgess capture what this book is intended to achieve. A large part of the content and arguments of the book is from my doctoral research that I carried out a while ago in the University of Manchester (UK). The elaboration of content and arguments in the chapters are also due to the courses on 'Children and Theologies' that I have been teaching at Bachelors and Masters level, most of which are published in my articles published in theological journals and volumes. My thanks to students of these courses who push the boundaries of my thought-process with their compelling interrogation of my arguments. I apply the principles of the research in Child-friendly and Child-centred Church workshops and Christian Education workshops in the Church of South India Synod projects and elsewhere. Thankfully, these thoughts have been well-received.

Sincere thanks are certainly due to my doctoral research supervisor in the University of Manchester Professor Rev. Peter M. Scott, Samuel Ferguson Professor of Applied Theology & Director of the Lincoln Theological Institute; to research panelists Dr. Susannah Cornwall, now Senior Lecturer in Constructive Theologies, University of Exeter, and Dr. Chris Shannahan, Associate Professor at Coventry University Centre for Peace, Trust, and Social Relations; and to my external examiner Dr. Anthony G. Reddie, Professor Extraordinarius, Department of Philosophy, Practical and Systemic

Theology at the University of South Africa, and the current Director of Oxford Centre for Religion and Culture of Regent's Park College, UK.

My research was possible by the generous Lincoln International Doctoral Studentship Fee Award from Lincoln Theological Institute based in the department of Religions and Theology in the University of Manchester. The Institute also provided me a plentiful travel grant for a field-research trip to India. I thank its Director Prof. Rev. Peter M. Scott and its Trustees for their constant encouragement and support.

Many thanks to the National Council of Churches in India which published my masters research on children, rights and Christian ministry in India, and to the Board of Theological Education of Senate of Serampore for publishing my resource book on Children as Risk and Inclusive Societies.

My wife Prof. Dr. Jayachitra Lalitha and son Pranay continue to give me the strongest support despite their own responsibilities and changing circumstances. My parents, sister's family, in-laws, relations, friends and wishers both in India and UK, especially in Manchester, have upheld me through the research journey and in my continued ministry. Very special mention must be made of Revd Dr Terry Biddington, the then Co-ordinating Chaplain to the Manchester Higher Education Community and the University Chaplaincy, for having me on the Chaplaincy team, which further connected me to ministries in church and local communities. I wish them all God's continued blessings and grace.

I am truly indebted to Mr. Sundhanshu Kanda for his continued encouragement and perceverance in bringing this book out. Many thanks to his staff too at CWI.

I gladly offer this work with the hope of a continued conversation in the best interest of children and childhood.

Rev. Dr. Rohan P. Gideon, M.A., M.Th., Ph.D
Professor, Christian Theology
The United Theological College
Bengaluru (India)

Preface

Following the unexpected and unprecedented reception of his book, *The Postmodern Condition: A Report on Knowledge* (1979, ET 1984), Jean-François Lyotard published a follow-up, with the English translation entitled *The Postmodern Explained: Correspondence 1982 – 1985* (ET 1992). I find it fascinating that the French original has the title *Le Postmoderne expliqué aux enfants* (1988), that is "The Postmodern explained to children." It is fascinating that the actual title regarding explaining postmodernism to children was probably deemed facetious by the English translation editors, leading to something which in my opinion does disservice to something deeply significant that Lyotard discerned and put up-front-and-centre, namely, that something as complex as postmodernism was, at the same time, something that was explainable and graspable by children. I recognize that one can easily quibble with this statement and I can hear readers saying, "let's read a short section of this book aloud to children and ask them what sense, if any, they made out of this"!! That is not the point – the point is that Lyotard consciously or unconsciously delved back into a fundamental but often dismissed insight of the Christian legacy and tradition, and that is Jesus' affirmation of children time and time again, as in his response to people when they brought "little children to him in order that he might touch them; and the disciples spoke sternly to them. But when Jesus saw this, he was indignant and said to them, 'Let the little children come to me; do not stop them; for it is to such as these that the kingdom of God belongs. Truly I tell you, whoever does not receive the kingdom of God as a little child will never enter it'" (Mark 10:13–15, NRSV).

It is to the credit of Rohan Gideon that children have been at the apex of his research, writings, commitments, and public ministry; they form the subject that he has explored, interrogated, and contributed to for many years, from examining the tragic work conditions of child labourers to exploring how Christianity had a different attitude to children from the very beginning as it emerged in the Roman world; from the conundrum of church structures and ministerial authorities treating children as "half-members" to certain strands of theology instrumentalizing children; from never underestimating the importance of solid and challenging Christian education from Sunday School onwards in local contexts to keeping abreast of the burgeoning field of "child studies" in the academy, as, for example, the "Childhood Studies and Religion Unit" of the American Academy of Religion, where the self-description of this on the AAR website reads: "The focus of the Unit is both timely and significant given the present concern for children across the globe and the rising interdisciplinary academic interest in childhood studies. The Unit functions as a forum at the AAR for advancing childhood studies as a new line of scholarly inquiry."

This book is a valuable and timely resource as the centrality and complexity of the child is recognized and valorized in theological reflection and pastoral praxis, the child, characterized and personified as poverty by the Dalit poet-activist, Namdeo Dhasal, in his poem "Sweet Baby Poverty" who writes:

… lift up this little one with all the care in the world.
It'll pee on your shirts, be watchful.
Child born of all our anguish, sweet baby poverty.

> [in his *A Current of Blood: Poems Selected and Translated from the Marathi by Dilip Chitre* (New Delhi: Navayana, 2010), p. 54].

In his call to a reinvigoration of theology through a rediscovery and a recommitment to the agency of the child, even when the adult-centric barriers seem impenetrable, what with adults seeing themselves as guardians restricting access to the numinous and failing to comprehend that the numinous has slipped by them and shines through children, Rohan Gideon forces us to confront our concretized prejudices, our smug certainties, our taken-for-granted convictions, and our easy dismissal of the strange ways in which truth unveils herself, especially when this emerges from those considered incapable of being the bearers of truth, those whom the Japanese theologian, Kagawa Toyohiko characterizes as "eternally innocent and eternally curious." [in "I Want to be a Child again," Kagawa Toyohiko, *A Few Words in the Dark*, trans. and annotated by Thomas John Hastings (Princeton, NJ: Bridges to Peace Publications, 2015), p. 114].

I write this during the season of Epiphany, when we are not just reminded of the "manifestation" of our "little Lord Jesus" but also are reminded of tyrannical authorities, in this case exemplified by King Herod, who felt so threatened by a newly-born baby that he ordered the destruction and annihilation of a whole group of innocent children in his realm. Perhaps it was these sibling-companions of the baby-Jesus whom he had in mind when, in response to a question regarding the most prominent in the kingdom of heaven, Jesus "called a child, whom he put among them, and said, 'Truly I tell you, unless you change and become like children, you will never enter the kingdom of heaven. Whoever becomes humble like this child is the greatest in the kingdom of heaven. Whoever welcomes one such child in my name welcomes me'" (Matthew 18:1–5, NRSV).

Rohan Gideon offers us much to think about, ponder upon, and act swiftly as we read this book and enable its flourishing in our theological, ecclesial, ministerial, and missional commitments that are informed by children and the Child.

- Rev. Dr. J. Jayakiran Sebastian
H. George Anderson Professor of Mission and Cultures and Former Dean
United Lutheran Seminary | Gettysburg + Philadelphia
United Lutheran Seminary

Recommendation

I am delighted to commend Rohan Gideon's interrogation of what he calls Child-focussed theologies in which he exposes their adult-centric basis. Justifying his approach by reference to liberation theological method, Gideon pays careful attention to the concept of agency and the resisted ascription of that agency to younger children. Grounding his analysis thereby is an account of the inviolable dignity of children, whatever their age. In turn, this requires a re-engagement with the traditions associated with Jesus which requires us to critique standard ways of referring only to the adult Jesus and failing to relate 'the child' to the divine. This is a highly promising line of argument that extends the liberation approach in creative ways across the binary of adult/child and thereby contends against a ubiquitous yet arbitrary restriction in human dignity. I strongly recommend this book.

Professor Rev. Dr. Peter M. Scott
Samuel Ferguson Professor of Applied Theology and Director
of the Lincoln Theological Institute
University of Manchester, Manchester (UK)

Introduction

In my quest to understand what advances the agency of the child both globally and in my own national context, India, I attempt to nuance the arguments of the agency of the child, the solidarity of the adults and the immanent mystery. The understanding of the agency of the agency of the child constitutes view, expressions that are both creative, reactionary and disruptive, and their very presence with their unsettling imagination. These constituent thoughts are sourced from histories, scriptures, theological expressions and from our cultural learnings, in both written and oral forms. The specific contexts of these arguments and understandings are Children-related theologies and liberationist theologies in India.

This work is a critical study of the inadequacies and untapped potentials of two methodological streams: methodologies of liberation theologies in India and methodologies of Child-focussed theologies in advancing an understanding of the agency of children. Liberation theologies in India have had reinvented liberationist principles to address the needs of dalits, women, tribals and adivasis.

Liberation theologies in India have been couched in the discourses that advance adult subjectivity and have not explored the possibility of understanding the agency of child in their methodologies. By contrast, many child-focussed theologies are currently attempting methods and explanations that seem to advance the agency of the child. Of them, two significant streams, Child theologies and Holistic Child Development, have been impacting theological thinking in India to claim the subjecthood of children with the aim of advancing the centrality of children and their agency. The child-focussed theologies have claimed to develop the concept of the agency of children by drawing methodological insights from liberation theologies. However, these children-related theologies have not adequately explored the hermeneutical principles of liberation theologies, thus falling short of contributing to the explanation of the agency of the child.

Chapter One presents the conundrums that children are in or exposed to in theological and social contexts. It discusses some theoretical debates on extremely resistant forms of agency among the adult subjects which would distance resources for liberation coming in the forms of advocacy and solidary. It also offers a methodological framework called 'qualitative agency' which opens up expansive spaces to explore intersectional interactions to place children in these discourses.

Chapter Two offers a critical appraisal of the 'child in the midst' method, a unique and creative method of contemporary child-focussed theologies which envisions to advance the agency of the children. The arguments assess where the child-focussed theologies have wavered and hesitated to explore liberationist theological principles after having claimed to initiated the application of these principles.

Chapter Three takes Christology as a case to explain how child-focussed theologies can draw insights both affirmative and cautious arguments from the life and teachings of Jesus and also from different christological debates. It explains that only bolder and unconventional forms of Christology help advance the agency of the child.

Chapter Four explains the strong influences of methodological exclusivism in Indian liberationist theologies which have left the themes of deeper solidarities less explored, thereby making these theologies unable to discover spaces to address the risks and vulnerabilities of children in Indian contexts. The chapter examines how postcolonial theoretical principles aids expand the liberative framework of the liberationist theologies in India.

Chapter Five explains that for the agency of the child to be recognized and advanced there should be purposeful and committed solidarity of adults at the expense of their adult-entitlement. The committed solidarity can be deeply strengthened and held together by exploring the belief in the Immanent mystery of the divine and the child.

Chapter 1

The Agency of the Child Theological and Social Conundrums

The arguments for advancing the agency of the child are made in a context where discussion and debates about children and theology are inhabited by adulthood-dominant mindsets and further reflected in adulthood-centric theological thoughts about God, Christ, agency, advocacy and liberation. More specifically, it is an exploration of the agency amidst the adult-dominance within the methodologies of our theologies including the burgeoning child-focussed theologies in the west and in Asia, namely Child theology, Holistic Child Development, and Theologies of Childhood. Even many liberation theologies that try to bring to the centre of the debates human communities that include children, exclude children as significant participants.[1] The adult-dominant situations emerge when people are categorized on the basis of age and age-related capacities in which the adults are able to control and colonize the minds and bodies of children in the pretext of socializing the children and help them towards a level of maturity, which is usually favourable to the adults. Here it is argued that for the agency of child to take form, manifest

[1] Rohan P. Gideon, *Child Labour in India: Its Challenges for Theological Thought and Christian Ministry in India* (Delhi/Nagpur: ISPCK/NCCI. 2011).

and thrive in unfavourable theological and cultural conditions, there must be a robustly supplementing understanding of 'rooted solidarity of the adults' along with a well thought through theology of the 'immanent mystery'. In a world that intimidates children at every possible level and instrumentalizes them, the agency of the children needs the rooted solidarity of the adult community. The combination of the agency of the child and the rooted solidarity can be theologically strengthened by recognizing the immanent mystery that is present in children while addressing the mystery of God and God's manifestations.

The last twenty years have seen a strident and focussed development of child-focussed theologies like Child theologies, Theologies of Childhood, and Holistic Child Development. These theologies have claimed to have more effective and progressive presentation of the centrality and agency of the child than their preceding discourses in Christian theology. Therefore, their intention is to see children as theological agents.

For the convenience of our understanding, I have devised the term 'Child-focussed theologies' as an umbrella term which covers the above theological streams. Many of the theological themes from these movements have explored the themes of agency, solidarity, liberation and their conundrums. More significantly, their method—the Child-in-the-Midst method, claims to interrogate adult-dominance in Christian theological thought. Through my analysis of the method, I argue that the Child-in-the-midst method of the child-focussed theologies continues to perpetuate an adult-centric approach both subtly and unswervingly albeit their claims to promote the subjectivity of children and their agency. Moreover, I argue that the child-focussed theologies have not adequately explored liberation theological method which they claim they subscribe to in their arguments. It is equally important to note that even liberation theologies carry age biases just as gender and other discriminatory biases.

The Agency of the Child: Some Immediate Situations and Questions

The understanding of the agency of the child considers the impact children make by their presence as social and political actors and also by their views and expression. These views and expressions emerge out of their endowed wisdom as complementing and supplementing the conversations, but also as fierce responses to the desecration of their rights and dignity. The agency of the child can be elucidated at two levels: i. children's capacity to express their views and opinions that affirms the wisdom endowed in them as human beings, and ii. their capacity to interrogate the difficult socio, cultural and political circumstances that affect their being and becoming. Both these understandings have the potential to raise new questions about our existential issues. Nuancing it further, acknowledging the capacity of children to define their agency must consider different age groups of children because of the period of exposure and socializing they have in their contexts. Children's suppressed subjectivity or agency emerges from a culture of socializing where there is a unilateral imposition of adult objectives on children. In such social contexts, opinions and experiences of children are ignored and neglected. For this reason, the understanding of the agency of the child should include children's presence and participation as much as their views and expression coming from certain knowledge systems endowed in them alongside their views that come from their suppressed subjectivity.

The views of Prout and James on agency as the action of choice or a spontaneous interaction leading to change[2] opens up the scope of the agency. The agency of the child also includes the act of children speaking up for their rights and dignity when they are conscientized of the context of the violation of their rights and being. The age and awareness of children about their dignity become an important analytical factor as children, especially those of lower ages are unaware of their rights and dignity and therefore do not realize the violation of their rights and their being.

The debates on children's agency considers children's participation in state politics through children's parliament and the

[2] Prout, A. & James A., "A New Paradigm for the Sociology of Childhood? Provenance, Promise and Problems, in *Constructing and Reconstructing Childhood: Contemporary Issues in Sociological Study of Childhood, Second edition* (London, Falmer Press, 1997), 7-33.

power of such debates in shaping the understanding of children's agency as co-partners with adults. Likewise, children are being included in designing the educational curriculum in regular schools and in churches education commonly known as Christian education. Therefore, a crucial debate is that children in adult-dominant institutions do not find prospects to demonstrate their agency. If at all, the agency of the child finds expression within the adult-controlled structures which largely reflect the adult language system. This has been discussed sociologically in the sociology of childhood.[3] Highlighting the structures as adult-dominant or adult-controlled does not mean that all adults are insensitive to the needs and agency of the child. Although coming with an adult-advantage, adults related to children through familial and other relationships advocate children's agency by questioning the adult structure they benefit from. Through such proactive participation, the adults recognize the need for spaces for children towards creative spaces of engagement and conversations. Also, a caution to be borne in mind is that the advocacy of adults could either constrain or enable the spaces for children's agency.

The explanation of agency is classically connected to social structures and how agency and social structure reciprocate in constituting or reconstituting each other. Discussions on agency gain prominence with a critical assessment of structuralism which either negate or diminish the role and actions of individuals as significant in shaping a discourse. The reasons for an agency are ascribed to two factors: to a structure where human agency is a consequence of its structural constraints or cultural stresses, and where human agency or action is a product of inherent wisdom and self-will. The inherent and self-willed agency can challenge a structure inadvertently.

A very important argument in this work is that advancing the agency of the child as an exclusive focus is challenging and complicated in a largely adult-centric world. The agency should be strongly complemented by rooted solidarity of adults and an appropriate understanding of the immanent mystery of God which

[3] James A., Jenks, C., and Prout A., *Theorising Childhood* (Cambridge, Polity Press, 1998).

is reflected in children. Where the adult-child dichotomy has been deliberately perpetuated in the name of culture, religion, theologies and social practices, the understanding of agency of the child defines social-construction, self-concept, and attitudes of being, relating and belonging. The Child-focussed theological discourses have concentrated their efforts on asserting the right of children to be heard in real terms to change the way the policies are children-friendly, children-inclusive and children-attentive. In doing so, locating children within the research community will move beyond making children an end in themselves to understanding children's lives and their relationships with their contexts as significantly contributing and crucial in meaning making.

A closest example to the debate of this nature can be found in one of the child-focussed theologies, Child theology, which reflects this struggle as it wrestles with questions such as: How might attention to children and childhood better help us to seek and understand and enter into and witness to God's kingdom? As a result, how might it prompt us to rethink or re-evaluate current understandings of central Christian beliefs and practices? Answers to these and more questions inform and lead to further theological debates to combine the triad of the agency of the child, the rooted solidarity of the adult community and the immanent mystery. Christologically speaking Jesus' own example, both as a child and his teachings as a preacher and practitioner act as pointers to the kingdom of God that unhesitantly include children. Therefore, the above questions need more qualifying explanations for a deeper understanding of the agency of the child.

Qualifying Principles for a Qualitative Agency

The understanding of the agency of the child has to be qualified in a context where children's voices reflect their own views and perspectives much in disapproval to the ongoing language of the dominant adults about children. This mishmash of the language system about children can be clarified by drawing critical principles from Simone Bignall's *qualitative agency* as explained in her work *Postcolonial Agency: Critique and Constructivism.* The qualitative agency decentres the role of the dominant and yet sees their constructive role in a postcolonial engagement in the light of the experiences of the colonized. The colonizer and the colonized engage in a conversation with different perspectives on the need to negotiate an agreeable resolution. This resolution could be short-term and context-specific. The qualitative agency facilitates a constructive engagement between the once colonizer and the colonized. The conversational principles are: overcoming conceptual difficulties towards a new sociability; a qualitative transformative possibility; identifying the creative potentials of the differences, and a positive connotation of power.[4]

Briefly, a clearer understanding of qualitative agency is by augmenting its hermeneutical quality in the presence of quantitative postcolonial agency. The quantitative agency has a strong language of political resistance to dominant structures. These forms of resistance challenge the colonizer-colonized binaries when the participants "act within, against, and according to a lasting legacy of colonial sociality."[5] Such resistance gives rise to newer forms of "internal colonisation."[6] However, qualitative agency offers a critique of the quantitative agency and propels towards a constructive notion of agency.

Bignall's proposal for a qualitative postcolonial perspective comes as an alternative to various forms of postcolonial interactions. She develops her thoughts from Felix Guattari and Gilles Deleuze, simultaneously interacting with and drawing insights critically from Foucault. Bignall's immediate context is the postcolonial debate

---

[4] Simone Bignall, *Postcolonial Agency: Critique and Constructivism* (Edinburgh: Edinburgh University Press, 2010).

[5] Simone Bignall, *Postcolonial Agency,* 2.

[6] Simone Bignall, "Deleuze and Foucault on desire and Power," *Angelaki: Journal of Theoretical Humanities* 13, no. 1 (2008): 128. In the recent decades, there have been an insistence on employing Foucauldian categories of agency and subjectivity to analyze the formative factors of liberationist theologies in India. At the core of this insistence is to affirm that individuals and oppressed communities do have voices: both endowed and resistant voices. Vinayaraj, Y. T. "Envisioning a Postmodern Method of doing Dalit Theology." In *Dalit Theology in the Twenty-first Century*, 93-103. New Delhi: Oxford University Press, 2010; Vinayaraj Y. T. *Revisiting the Other: Discourses on Postmodern Theology.* Tiruvalla: Christava Sahitya Samithi, 2010. Elaborate discussions of these dynamics are in chapter 4.

in Australia which seeks reconciliation between indigenous and non-indigenous communities. What is her image of a postcolonial context? It is a context in which "bodies occupy the same territory; each experiences a significant sense of belonging."[7] The sense of belonging is also an act of reconciliation because belonging is a "process of becoming compatible drawing from a 'common concept' of the postcolonial…"[8] For Deleuze, it is an "ontological becoming" through which one could envision a different view of self and unfolds into an "open-ended process of actualisation that has an immanent cause."[9] Bignall seeks compossibility in the context of reconciliation. In the process she attempts to see both the colonised as well as the coloniser working out a postcolonial agency from a "common concept." Bignall considers a historically postcolonial Australian context but that which does not create an engaging space for the once colonized aboriginals to express their views to stake their claim for greater reconciliation and their agency in state policies. Through this, Bignall rereads Deleuze and Guattari arguing that their proposal reinstates a postcolonial type of reconciliation which is "not as progressive unification, but as the collective enactment of a historical discontinuity."[10] Bignall calls this a qualitative perspective.

Bignall's qualitative perspective defines social construction, self-concept, attitudes of being, relating and belonging; therefore, she proposes an ethical mode of interaction which is more conversational and interactive. Bignall builds on a general notion of agency that considers human capacity to act or respond as crucial. Significantly, the qualitative agency deals with the colonizer-colonized binary by retrieving the agency of the colonized as well as recognizing the "responsibility and transforming capacity of formerly colonizing subjects."[11] This can be achieved by a] overcoming the colonized-colonizer binary towards a new sociability. Historically, the postcolonial emphasis was exclusively or predominantly on

[7] Bignall, "Deleuze and Foucault," 141.

[8] Bignall, "Deleuze and Foucault," 141.

[9] Bignall, *Postcolonial Agency,* 9.

[10] Bignall, *Postcolonial Agency,* 9.

[11] Bignall, *Postcolonial Agency,* 4.

the question of the agency of the colonized. Later, in the course of addressing the issues of the agency of the colonized, a new sociability in qualitative agency also addressed the agency of the former colonizers who offer their liberative resources to participate in a new sociability. New sociability also presupposes creating flexible configurations of social structures to continue the engagement which in turn supports the social structure; b] a qualitative transformative possibility: a qualitative transformative possibility is a postcolonial practice that recognizes the capacity of the colonizer to identity the dominant legacy and transforms it to an exercise of relationships. The transformation overcoming the conceptual difficulties that avoids the dangers of a extremes like an identity-specific exclusivist position or a grand homogenous unity. It opens up spaces to welcome new bodies towards new engagements. It presumes the colonizer psychologically decolonizing oneself from the benefits of imperial legacy and translating it into an act of transforming society. Explaining this about the colonizing adult mindset, the adults exercise their capacity to realize the matrix of dominance they create which endangers the identity of children. They also exercise intergenerational interactions through policies and theologies; c] Identifying the creative potentials of the differences: In a situation where differences are taken advantage of to recreate hierarchies, the objective of this factor is to neither recreate another hierarchy based on power differentials nor to eliminate marginal values that the differences project. Rather, the awareness of the differences leads to new transformations. For a continually engaging postcolony, the differences should be allowed to be "critical" and "creative potential", and not just otherness in a negative sense. However, the understanding of otherness should not be restricted to the socially marginal. Explaining this for children's colonized situation, children's potentials are recognised by freshly reunderstanding the image of God in children, a sense of ontological mystery that is in and surrounds humanity especially children and also to emphasize the real voices of children in rights violated contexts; and d] a positive connotation of power: A positive understanding of power in qualitative agency envisions new transformations and maintains the differences between the colonized and coloniser. The differences are maintained purposefully to explore their strengths and to exhibit a constant need for relationships. A positive understanding of power constitutes their desire for new relationships, their capacity to unsettle imperial notions of relationships, and their reflexivity to create more agentic spaces for the colonized.[12]

The Agency of the Child and Theological Conundrums

The methodologies of liberation theologies in India and children-related theologies have shown inadequacies to advance an understanding of the agency of the child. Liberation theologies in India have been adult-centric discourses and have not explored the possibility of understanding the agency of the child in their methodologies. These methodologies are methodological exclusivism, methodological inclusivism and praxis. Liberation theologies in India have addressed the pressing need for the agency of marginalized adults such as dalits, women, and tribals amidst the violation of their agency. However, their hermeneutical principles have been inadequate to interrogate the silenced agency of the child especially in the context of the gross violation of child-rights.[13]

By contrast, the child-focussed theologies are currently attempting methods and explanations that seem to advance the agency of the child. Of them, two significant streams, Child theologies and Holistic Child Development, have been impacting theological thinking to claim the subjecthood of children with the aim of advancing the centrality of children and their agency. The child-focussed theologies have claimed to develop the concept of the agency of the child by drawing methodological insights from liberation theologies. However, these children-related theologies have not adequately explored the hermeneutical principles of liberation theologies, thus falling short of contributing to an explanation of the agency of the child. Two methodological positions of the child-focussed theologians need to be interrogated: a] why are the Child theologians cautious or less persuasive in deploying the hermeneutics of liberation theologies to enhance the possibility of the agency of the

---

[12] Bignall, *Postcolonial Agency*, 4-20.

[13] Rohan P. Gideon, *Child Labour in India.*

child? and, b] what reconfiguration of liberationist methodological principles, which are available but not effectively employed by children related theologians, facilitate a renewed understanding of the agency of the child in adult-dominant discourses?

In the debates on the agency in modern and postmodern philosophy that have influenced the liberation theological movement, the contentious issue has been the location of the agency in the agency-structure debate. These debates have strongly influenced the concept of the agency of the marginalized in Indian liberation theologies such as dalit theology, womanist theology, feminist theology and tribal theology. These theologies discuss the renewed subjectivity that enhances the agency of the marginalized communities as well as individuals who could continually negotiate their postcolonial identity. However, the dangerous proposition for children's agency is that the subjectivity of children could be lost in the adult-centric context. Therefore in the attempt to define the agency of the child, it is crucial to explain how dominant adults could advocate on behalf of the agency of the child. This will be unique to the child-focussed theologies as the above-mentioned theologies are adult-centric theologies. Moreover, a significant contribution to the themes of the agency of the child is the theological nuances of the notion of mystery.

To understand how the child-focussed theologies and Indian liberation theologies interact methodologically, the child-focussed theologies have demonstrated a tactical acquiescence to liberation theologies. They theologies have made two claims: firstly, they are along the lines of liberation theologies to assert the subjectivity of children and secondly the child-in-the-midst method of Child theologies presents an overarching explanation for the centrality of children and their agency. Therefore, children-related theologies in principle project the centrality of children as their core objective[14] but do not press further to claim the significance of children's agency.

As its limitations, the objective of the the child-focussed theologies as liberation theologies has not been explored widely

[14] John Collier ed., *Toddling to the Kingdom: Child Theology at Work in the Church* (London: Child Theology Movement, 2009).

for several reasons. Firstly, they are emerging disciplines and they have been exploring liberationist hermeneutics on how to explain the unique voices of children and at the same time clarify the understanding of adult advocacy. Secondly, even as they explore the unique voices of children, they are tentative and cautious in pursuing their claims. This, I argue, is because their prospective projection of the child as an agent of theology could displace what/who many child-theologians call the central subject: Jesus Christ and his kingdom values. Therefore, the agency of the child as projected in the child-focussed theologies take a less significant place than hermeneutically essential. While the central idea of the child-focussed theologies is to advance the agency of the child, the views of children are expected to be represented by adults.[15] Jan Grobbelaar attempted to consider the liberationist mode of interpretation for the child-focussed theologies and to a great extent proposed a projection of the voices and views of children alongside the advocacy of the adults.[16] However, the discussion on the advocacy of adults is dubious as the explanations for the agency of the child are carefully couched in adult-dominant language. Therefore, the child-focussed theologies are largely silent on children's views as children's own agency. Moreover, the agency of the child is discussed in abstract terms without seriously considering context-specific issues. White even mentions that

[15] Keith White, "The Child in the Midst of the Biblical Witness," in *Toddling to the Kingdom: Child Theology at Work in the Church*, ed. John Collier (London: Child Theology Movement, 2009), 154-160; Keith White, "Thinking about Child Theology in the context of Liberation Theologies" (Paper presented at the Oxford Centre for Mission Studies, Oxford, November 30, 2010), 6-7; Sunny Tan, *Child Theology* for *the Churches in Asia: An Invitation* (London: Child Theology Movement, 2007); Jesudason B. Jeyaraj, "Child in the Midst: Incarnation and Child Theology," in *Children at Risk: Issues and Challenges*, eds. Jesudason B. Jeyaraj *et al* (Delhi: ISPCK, 2009), 49-72; Rohan P. Gideon, *Child Labour in India: Its Challenges for Theological Thought and Christian Ministry in India* (Delhi/Nagpur: ISPCK/NCCI. 2011).

[16] Jan Grobbelaar, *Child Theology and the African Context* (London: Child Theology Movement Ltd., 2012).

contextual issues are not always relevant while discussing the centrality of children.[17]

It is evident that the child theologies in the west project a rather restrained approach to the liberationist stance. This restrained and tentative approach raises potential challenges in understanding the agency of the child: *firstly*, as a limitation, the child-focussed theologies under-explore the concept of the agency of the marginalized that are presented in liberation theologies in India and *secondly*, their cautious approach to the advocacy of adults underscores their hesitation to pursue the understanding of the agency of the child.

In the context of Indian Christian liberation theologies, it must be noted that the agency of dalits in dalit theology, the agency of women in feminist and womanist theologies and the agency of tribals in tribal theology have effectively transformed the modes of theologizing. By advancing their agency, the historically marginalized have not attempted to displace the concept of God or Jesus Christ but deeply explore the subjectivity of the marginalized caste, tribal and patriarchal structures. Clearly, liberation theologies provide strong hermeneutical directions to the child-focussed theologies in ways to not eclipse Jesus Christ from their theological propositions.

With Christological prejudices in child-focussed theologies, an analysis of internal colonies in liberation theologies and children-related theologies offer us methodological and hermeneutical insights towards incorporating the agency of the child in Indian theological contexts as much as in the broader theological debates. These discussions help the child-focussed theologies to further explore the concept of the agency of the child as a marginalized and colonized group alongside the concept of the agency of the marginalized in the liberation theologies.

---

[17] Keith White, "Thinking about Child Theology in the Context of Liberation Theologies" (paper presented at the Oxford Centre for Mission Studies, Oxford, November 30, 2010).

The Agency of the Child and Contextual Conundrums

Postcolonial philosopher Edward Said gives a fresh perspective to the ambiguous relationship between subjectivity and agency. Said develops his idea of subjectivity from Foucault's disapproval of the precedence of truth to knowledge, a Cartesian standard.[18] Said finds Foucault's ideas on subjectivity problematic because Foucault's rejection of truth-based knowledge is not enough to separate agency from subjectivity. For Said, power works in relationships and it is wilfully used or abused. This is in contrast to Foucault's presentation of power which works in structures which are "impersonal [and] anonymous."[19] Therefore, Said is critical of Foucault's vagueness of the description of power which otherwise is manifest "physically and politically". In Said's words,

> What he [Foucault] seemed not as quite willing to grant is, in fact, the relative success of counter discursive attempts first to show the misrepresentations of discursive power, to show, in Fanon's words, the violence done to physically and politically repressed inferiors in the name of an advanced culture, and afterwards to begin the difficult, if not always tragically flawed project of formulating the discourse of liberation.[20]

For Said, the agency of the colonized manifests in a historical context. At a broader level, Said argues that purpose of agency is to be tangential in specific political and cultural contexts especially of the colonized. Such an agency offers the ability to reformulate interactions between different members of the structure with agentic significance to negotiate power practically.

Our contexts present children who face the challenges of life with varying degrees of oppressions or privileges. While on one hand there is a burgeoning movement to advance the agency

---

[18] Karlis Racevskis, "Edward Said and Michel Foucault: Affinities and Dissonances," *Research in African Literatures* 36, No. 3 (2005): 84.

[19] Edward W. Said, *Reflections on Exile and Other Literary and Cultural Essays* (London: Granta Books, 2001), 243-244.

[20] Said, *Reflections on Exile,* 243-244.

of the child, yet there is a negative sense to highlight and sustain adult-child binary. When the agency, of the child and solidarity of adults, who seek to advance the agency of the child, is caught up in an adult-dominant discourse, it pits the objective of reconciliation against differences as problematic. The difference as problematic is precisely what a positive desire for agency seeks to eradicate or alter. When the negated group of children acts to alter the situation or work out a liberative agency through its own embedded notions of agency, the negativity of differences among the adults silently let go off the accountability and apathy of the dominant.

As a classic example of the above paradox, Sarada Gopalan[21] illustrates an important debate in India that has strongly influenced the definition of the subjectivity and agency of the child in education-child labour debate. Balagopalan argues that the paradox of the colonial educational system in India strongly and less-critically promotes the traditional caste and class system. She also draws a connection, albeit indirectly, to the theological understanding of the adult-children binary by explaining how missionaries promoted technical education through educational institutions, thus strongly continuing the caste-education-Christian religious traditions.[22] A brief analysis of the debate demonstrates how the themes of children's agency, deep solidarity of adults, and mystery reconfigure at the intersections of theological, socio-cultural and political discourses and influence the understanding of the agency of the child.

By definition, children, whose agency is at risk, are persons under 18 years of age who experience an intense and/or chronic risk factor, or a combination of risk factors in personal, environmental and/or relational domains that prevent them from pursuing and fulfilling their God-given potential.[23] Another key distinction

---

[21] Sarada Balagopalan, *Inhabiting 'Childhood': Children, Labour and Schooling in Postcolonial India* (London: Palgrave Macmillan, 2014).

[22] Sarada Balagopalan, *Inhabiting 'Childhood'*, 67.

[23] Glenn Miles and Tony Senewiratne as quoted in McDonald, Patrick, and Emma Garrow. *Reaching Children in Need.* Eastbourne, UK: Kingsway Publications, 2000.

between all children and children-at-risk is to say that all children are inherently vulnerable by virtue of their developmental capacities and associated social influence relative to adults, but not all children are at socio-political and religious risks as those from lower rungs of caste, class and religions in our country. While the healty infants are still vulnerable to infancy-related issues and exposures, the genuinely responsible adults will work towards placing the more vulnerable infants at as lesser risks as possible. The mention of children-at-risk brings to our mind such children as homeless (i.e. street children or runaways), child labourers or those sexually exploited. Yet, while these types of categories are helpful to raise awareness and motivate action, there is a danger of developing generic narratives that could homogenize or not bear consequences to the complex life-situations of children. Instead, the overlapping and messy social challenges that children who are at risk face interrogate any easy categorization and ways and means of identifying the solutions for the problems.

Nearly 8 billion people are living in the world, including 2.2 billion children (aged 0-18), amongst them millions of children and young people without parental care or at risk of losing it. They are the most vulnerable and marginalized group. More than Around 70 percent of all children live in two continents, Asia and Africa. Statistics show that the number of children without parental care is rising. Today, there are an estimated 151 million children worldwide who have lost one or both parents, with at least 13 million of these children having lost both parents (about 10%).[24]

The complexity of missing voices of children intensifies when the discussion on the agency of the child is posited in context of child labour and its debate alongside the educational system in India. This is the context in India where the agency of the child is most violated, and where the adults who are expected to be the responsible advocates violate the dignity and subjecthood of children.

---

[24] *Child at Risk: The World's most Vulnerable Children: who they are, where they Live, and what puts them at Risk* https://www.sos-childrensvillages.org/getmedia/384bc38a-62aa-4c2a-9563-a5ecc61b6a77/SOS-Child-at-risk-freport-web.pdf

Postcolonial discourses on children and childhood exposes context-specific modes of colonisation and the need to engage at different levels conversations between the colonized and the colonizers in those specific contexts. It also interrogates homogenizing tendency of a community. Children in India are not a homogenous community. Indian context alerts us to the danger of homogenizing children community as they are separated on the basis of caste, class, gender and economic globalisation. Caste discourse in India, as critiqued in dalit theology, sees class, gender and neo-colonial forms of economic movements like globalisation as establishing and developing internal dynamics that eventually shape the caste discourse. A case study of child labour in Indian captures these dynamics to show that the communities of children in India cannot be homogenized as they are largely born and socialized into different caste categories influenced by other cultural movements.

In this section, I briefly present the conundrums that postcolonial India has carried forward from the erstwhile colonial times without critically examining the colonial biases that silence children's voices in many dominant discourses. These conundrums have been uncritically inherited by liberation theologies by being guilefully led into adult-dominant discourses. The education-labour debate in postcolonial India offers insights into where the agency of the child gets misplaced in Indian context and where adult-advocacy could be immensely necessary but with advocacy leading the adults to deeper solidarity. The debate on the children in regular educational systems as against child labour creates crucial discursive spaces to see how the immanent agency of the child is seen in shallow binary oppositions. On the one hand, the educational systems are deemed to present the best situation of the awareness of the rights and the agency of the child whereas on the other the children in labour are deemed completely devoid of their subjectivity and agency. Such circumstances are more than just binary oppositions or, as Nieuwenhuys call it, a "paradox". Niewenhuys argues that the governments, while condemning the relatively uncommon forms of waged labour as exploitation, sanctioned a broad spectrum of other activities like house-keeping, child minding, helping adults for no pay, working in family farms and shops, delivering newspapers, and seasonal works in farms and workshops. This establishes a borderline between morally desirable and pedagogically sensible activities on one hand, and the exploitation of children on the other.[25] The paradox also highlights that the rights-based society propagates education-debate without exposing the limitations of the rights debate. It is a paradox that human rights generally apply to full-fledged citizens and, children are not sufficiently recognized as full citizens.

The paradoxes about children's contextual lives and their place in state policies get more complex and complicated. Shelly Wright explains how women, children and indigenous peoples have usually not been treated as full citizens. Because of this invisibility, they suffer through inadequate recognition in international economic policies. While children in labour contribute to the state economy like any adult, they are deprived of protection by law for various types of violation of rights they undergo. The seriousness of these issues is much deeper.[26] Sheila Nair discusses that human rights do not investigate the links between global capital and human rights violations.[27]

There is clear data to show that the class-caste-minority religious community nexus continues to force the younger members of the family to work to make ends meet. In its latest observation, the commission has sharpened its focus on the age group and observes the presence of nearly 7% children below 14 years of age

---

[25] "The Paradox of Child Labour and Anthropology," The Oxford India Companion to Sociology and Anthropology, Veena Das. (New Delhi: Oxford University Press, 2003), 940- 941.

[26] Shelley Wright explains the discriminatory approach of the policy-making bodies in defining "human rights" and a "Citizen". She says that any unified and potential sovereign subject is the holder of rights. Therefore either single person or group- communities (with uniformity of identity) can claim human rights. However, 'abnormality' of gender, age, class, physical and mental "deviants" have been neglected in policy matters. See her International Human Rights, Decolonization and Globalization: Becoming Human (London: Routledge, 2001), 24-25, 62, 215, especially Ch. 4, "Subjects, Soldiers and Citizens."

[27] Sheila Nair, "Human Rights and Postcoloniality," in Power, Postcolonialism and International Relations: Reading Race, Gender and Clas, 256-258.

in the above-mentioned labour force, while the presence of children between the ages of 15-19 is a glaring 39%.[28]

Here, two dynamics should not escape our attention. Firstly, and obviously, the glaring difference between the percentage of children in the labour force between two cut-off age-groups, i.e., 14 years and 19 years shows the ugly haste of exploitative forces to push children to labour force once they have reached the legally safe age of 15. While it is 7% below 14 years, it is a pole-apart 39% between 15-19 years. Secondly, this analysis confirms the view that children from most marginalized communities are forced into the labour sector and are deprived of the basic rights of compulsory education and a healthy and playful childhood. These facts make it imperative for our theologies to take up the issues of child labour with unreserved commitment and absolute seriousness.

Postcolonial India continues to practice caste and class politics which has deep significance in the understanding of children in India and their agency. One of the deplorable practices where the agency of the child is violated is in the practice of child labour. The overwhelming majority (around 85%)[29] of child labourers in India comes from communities and groups which are at the lower rungs of the traditional, caste-based social hierarchy, i.e., the Scheduled castes, Scheduled Tribes, Other Backward Classes and minorities, especially Muslims. This amounts to the majority of the Indian population.[30]

Interestingly the history of domination in Indian Christian theology is a glaring reflection of the socio-historical context of India albeit the difference at the statistical level. In the larger Indian context, dalits are a minority dominated over by a larger socio-religious group. However, among the Christian population, dalits are the majority, yet being dominated by the higher groups in the caste hierarchy even within the Christian church and its theologies.

[28] National Commission for Enterprise in the Unorganised Sector, 48.

[29] Azadi India Foundation, *Child Labour in India,* http://azadindia.org/social-issues/child-labour-in-india.html (14 November, 2011).

[30] Encyclopaedia of Child and Family Welfare - Vol. 4, 141. Also see, Manoranjan Mohanty, *Class, Caste, Gender*, 20.

This intriguing dynamic indicates a conundrum that to address the colonial structure within the confines of Christian theology, Christian theologians have to not only be aware of the wider colonial dynamics and their implication but also negotiate their way through the maze of caste systems in the context of many religions. To add to it is the sub-caste dynamics which are again different in different regions of the country.

Education versus Child Labour Debate

The traditional caste-stratified society that India has been with its history of being colonized by western civilization has either directly or indirectly silenced children or disregarded their presence. The caste system itself is an India variety of colonization legitimized by religious scriptures. Children from the marginalized castes and related classes have historically been vulnerable and have been at risk in the present context. Therefore, it interrogates any form of homogenizing tendency of a community. Any notion of children in India is a homogenous community is contestable. Indian context alerts us to the danger of homogenizing the children community as they are separated on the basis of caste, class, gender and economic globalisation. Caste discourse in India—as discussed in dalit theology—sees class, gender, and neo-colonial forms of economic movements like globalisation as establishing and developing internal dynamics that eventually shape the caste discourse. A case study of child labour in Indian captures these dynamics to show that the communities of children in India cannot be homogenized as they are largely born and socialized into a caste category.

It is a common knowledge that India has the largest number of child labourers in the world.[31] The deliberations on child labour, being situated at the intersections of economic, cultural, legal, religious, and social institutions, have eluded attempts to comprehend, address and confront the phenomenon of child labour. These intersections are perceived not only as the determinants of the

---

[31] Avtar Singh, "Child Labour Problems and Prospects: Socio-Legal Measures," *Social Action* Vol. 54, No. 4 (Oct-Dec), 396-97. Most of the literature on Child Labour, especially of Child Labour in India, attests to this fact.

economic activity like child labour but also as the ones "producing and circulating meanings" and identities of the labouring children. Another intriguing challenge is to comprehend and evaluate the sector that child labour conceptually comes under: the Unorganised Sector or the Informal Sector.[32] Prakash Louis observes that being in the workforce of unorganized sector is not only an economic reality but also social and political in the Indian context. Most of the workers of informal sector come from the Dalit, Tribal, minority and most backward caste communities. It is this reality that escapes many social scientists who examine this phenomenon. Caste, class, ethnicity and gender are fundamental contributing factors to analyze the work force in the unorganised sector. Since the ruling elite comes from the dominant communities, it has no political will to address these issues. Rural- urban bias is another factor one has to observe in this sector.

Child Labour and Illiteracy Debate

Some commonly cited arguments for the families not sending their children to school is "inadequate schools", "lack of schools", or even "the expense of schooling" and therefore leaving some children with little else to do but work. Nearly 53.95 million children did not attend school in 1999-2000 which converts to 27.32 per cent of the child population between five to 14 years of age. In India, the 1999-2000 National Sample Survey (NSS) data indicate a high incidence of child labour, with 8.4 million children active in the labour force.[33] If the wider definition of child labour is accepted, which is that all

---

[32] The features that characterized unorganized work include lack of regulation of employment, seasonality of employment, denial of benefits under the labour laws, lack of social security protection and the absence of an employer-employee relationship. The reasons to so disorganise the labour is due to evasion of tax as well as excessive governmental regulation of market sector. Siddhartha Sarkar, "Theorizing in Informal Sector: Concept and Context," *Social Action* Vol. 54, No. 4 (Oct.-Dec. 2004): 359-373; Supriya Roy Chowdhury, "Globalization and Labour," *Economic and Political* 39/4 (Jan. 3 2004), 105; NCC Review CXXVII/7 (Aug. 2007), under the theme: 'Labour and Life in India'; Prakash Louis, "Editorial," *Social Action* vol. 54, No. 4 (Oct.-Dec.), iv-v.

[33] Azadi India Foundation, *Child Labour in India,* http://azadindia.org/social-issues/child-labour-in-india.html (August 2015).

the children who do not attend school should be counted as child labour, the incidence of child labour is enormous.

Varying attitudes of parents also contribute to child labour: some parents feel that children should work in order to develop skills useful in the job market instead of taking advantage of a formal education. The vicissitudes of rural agricultural and non-agricultural work and the schedule of schools do not necessarily preclude school-going children from working for wages or in family occupations. Schools, which could be a source to wean children off the labour market and put them through a process of learning, skill enhancing would not implement the necessary objectives.

Shanta Sinha argues that if the official sources put the figure of child labour at 17 million and those not attending schools in the 5-14 age-group are nearly 74 million, the government's schemes and legislations on child labour would cater only to those 17 million. Her contention is that these school dropouts are never "idle" but are invariably drawn into various forms of household labour but are deprived of the attention and benefits promised by the schemes and legislations. Therefore, they are missing children, and any later legislation would ignore their presence as child labourers.[34]

The education-labour debate presents heterogeneous categories of children in postcolonial India. These categories are caste, class, age, and urban or rural. The heterogeneity presents children from a class of families who can afford education as a means of developing their agency. Their caste and class backgrounds and their family heritage contribute and advocate largely to their desire to gain their agency. This is in stark contrast to those children who are driven to labour by their parents' societal constraints. We have seen that children in labour sector largely come from dalit and other backward caste groups confirming that the traditional caste-class nexus practices are still strong in driving children to labour. Therefore, it is noticeable that caste and class factors should be considered as crucial for discussion while formulating

[34] Shanta Sinha, "Child Labour and Education." Seminar 474 (Feb. 1999): 15-16.

an understanding of the agency of the child along the lines of liberation theologies.

However, we also noticed the down side of liberation theologies while addressing caste issues that could be overcome for children-related theologies. Dalit theology had so far emphasised adult-pathos as the norm. This research has explained that children's pathos is as significant in reformulating its idea of children's agency and subjectivity. To develop a self-critique method, liberation theologies could move from their earlier notion of historically motivated post-colonialism to a broader view of self-critiquing postcolonialism. Only then liberation theologies would be able to see the dominant ideology build into its discourse.

Problematising the understanding of children through education-labour debate provides clear indications on how liberation theologies in India and the child-focussed theologies could reassess their discussions on subjectivity and agency of the colonized. In all these discourses, one can notice elaborate discussions on the technicalities surrounding the economic issues in the labour market *sans* human face. Geetha Chowdhry contends that comprehending child labour as an economic process also "requires an examination of the production and circulation of commodities as well as meanings."[35]

Balagopalan rightly sees that the agency of the child is being absorbed into the discourse of the subjectivity of children. She explains that circumstances of children in streets and child labourers, who have not taken up basic education, complicate our understanding of childhoods that are fluidly constructed between the discourses of education and labour. The education-labour debate is trapped in adult and colonial discourses. Balagopalan states that just as in colonial India where the educational system "naturalized" the labouring skills of the families that the children came from, the current schooling systems too are drawn by "colonial modernity" that largely see children inherit the wisdom of caste and labouring categories that their parents did.[36] She adds:

[35] Geeta Chowdhry, "Postcolonial Interrogations," 227.

[36] Balagopalan, *Inhabiting 'Childhood'*, 60-61.

> More significantly, the state managed to advance this agenda—of reproducing caste and class hierarchies through schooling—by deploying the language of liberal benevolence, which was their sympathetic identification with what they perceived as native adult 'preference' for children's continued immersion in labour. And as this 'preference' was far from true, these efforts largely failed to deliver the desired results.[37]

Balagoplan examines the startling turnaround that caught the British colonial system by its own educational system in pre-Independence India that started to strike a balance between education and labour. The British system was taken aback when it noticed that more children from lower castes joined schools that Christian missionaries had started. Balagoplan explains again:

> Their [children of lower castes] increased enrolment, as noted in various official reports, sat uneasily with the growing recognition by the colonial state that for most lower-caste children, entry into modern schools affirmed the possibility of a different future outside of manual work... Schooling as that which served less 'as a means to improving a boy's mind so that he might bring more intelligence to his hereditary occupation of agriculture but as leading to some small post in which literacy was required' was for the colonial state a terrifying prospect.[38]

The empowered and educated children started to seek and claim jobs outside their traditional caste-based labour contradicting the expectation of the missionaries. The educational objectives of the missionary schools were to provide them with a basic education and so to make the children skilled in their own caste-based occupation. Therefore, the caste-class nexus is clearly shown to have been entrenched in the educational system. Through this educational system, the western colonial powers in India were to preserve the caste-class nexus.

---

[37] Balagopalan, *Inhabiting 'Childhood'*, 61.

[38] Balagopalan, *Inhabiting 'Childhood'*, 68.

As much as it is significant to identify the views and expressions of children in colonial contexts, it is also important to identify the advocating role of adults as the adult-dominant world is the colonizing factor for children. Such identification implies the recognition of the colonial state that children continue to be in and the same time identify a way forward for an intergenerational interaction. A significant step further in this discussion is to identify the immanent mystery in children as a positive factor that enhances the understanding of their agency. This theological factor gives an edge over other non-theological discourses in Indian context where religious discourse plays a significant role in advancing or diminishing the agency of the colonized.

Chapter 2

The Child-focussed Theologies and Liberationist Methods

The child-focussed theologies[39] have offered new ways forward in our understanding of the agency of the child through their method the Child-in-the-midst. However, these robust explanations have been located within a restricted framework of liberationist theological principles. This chapter engages with the robustness of the understanding of the agency of the children and highlights where the child-focussed theologies have been found wanting in their deeper understanding of the liberationist principles.

Marcia Bunge, a pioneer of Child Theology Movement, offers a broad outline for an understanding of centrality and significance of children through her comparison of Child theologies to liberationist theological streams such as feminist and black theologies. Child theology, as she sees it,

---

[39] Two types of resource mining have helped flesh out this work. Firstly, reviews of literature in the child-focussed theologies such as Child theologies in the west, Child theology in Asia, and Holistic Child Development. Secondly, interviews with some scholars of child-focussed theologies. There is not much literature published in this field. So I conducted one-to-one interviews these scholars in different parts of the world through email correspondences, skype and in person.

> re-examines not only conceptions of children and obligations to them but also fundamental doctrines and practices of the church. Drawing on analogies to feminist, black and liberation theologies, Child theologies have as their task not only to strengthen the commitment to and understanding of a group that has often been voiceless, marginalized and oppressed—children—but also to reinterpret Christian theology and practice as a whole.[40]

Bunge's proposal of the Child theology being on the lines of liberationist thoughts finds support in the views of other child theologians too, albeit with varying interpretative schemes. However, the central hermeneutical significance, which is the experience of children as being central to defining the agency of the child, has been retained. Another exponent of Child theology, John Collier, does not explicitly mention about the experience of children as the key hermeneutical principle, yet confirms Bunge's thoughts when he says,

> Child theology is akin to new theologies that have brought new questions to the Bible based on the experiences of those who had long been marginal to formal reflection: the poor, the women, the marginalized races that have brought to us liberation, feminine and black theologies… Children are the most oppressed social group.[41]

Keith White and Haddon Willmer, two ardent proponents of Child theology, reiterate the agentic power of children to alter the way we think and do theology when they say,

> As the poor transformed theology in Liberation Theology, and as women transform it in feminist theologies, so in

---

[40] Marcia J. Bunge, "Theologies of Childhood and Child theologies: International Initiatives to Deepen Reflection on Children and Childhood in the Academy and Religious Communities," *Dharma Deepika* 28/12/2 (July-December, 2008): 35.

[41] Collier, preface, 8-9.

> child theology it is the impact of the child that transforms theology.[42]

Further on the application of Child theology to contextual needs, Jaan Grobbelaar, a South African theologian, states that Child theology intends a key element of liberation theology, *praxis,* when he explains that Child theology "does not just seek new knowledge and understanding of God and God's way of doing things but a new way of living *with* children Coram Deo."[43] Child theology shares an important characteristic of liberation theology which is to learn life and practice "than a module in theology to be studied and applied." This learning key is drawn from Clodovis Boff, a Brazilian Roman Catholic liberation theologian.[44] Bunge too suggests this mode of analysis, but more at a conceptual level:

> By using the lens of the child, or by 'foregrounding' the child, Child theologies will be able to offer new insights into central themes of Christian faith and practice, such as God, creation, Christology, theological anthropology, sin, salvation, faith, the Word, worship, prayer, sacraments, missiology, and eschatology.[45]

With this proposal, Bunge opens up the scope of the impact of children and childhood on the theological thought process through the child-focussed theologies. Thus, Child theologies will build on strong theologies of childhood but have a broader scope.

It becomes evident that the child-focussed theologies are left with the task of further conceptualizing and elaborating the themes of solidarity and commitment of the adult-community to the communities of children that have often been voiceless and ineffectively represented before reinterpreting Christian theological themes doctrines and related practices.

---

[42] White and Willmer, "Our Response", 19.

[43] Italics mine. Grobbelaar, *Child Theology,* 18.

[44] Grobbelaar, *Child Theology,* 18.

[45] Bunge, "The Child, Religion, and the Academy." 569.

Various understandings and interpretations of the agency of the child need revisiting in the child-focussed theologies. The reviews here are about the significant methodological proposition introduced in the child-focussed theologies called the *Child-in-the-midst* method. This chapter is an analysis of this method that claims to bring to the centre of theological discourse children's subjectivity and potentially their agency.

Child theologies in Asia are largely influenced by the Child theologies in the west while Holistic Child Development has drawn both from the Child theologies in the west and liberation theological methods with a sense of urgency to discuss the centrality of the agency of the child. The following are various expressions of implicit and explicit adult-dominance under three themes as explored by different theologians from three different contexts: 'the Child-in-the-Midst: a silent and symbolic child' by Keith White and Haddon Willmer from European or western context, 'the Child-in-the-Midst: children in contexts' by Jan Grobbelaar from African context, and 'the Child-in-the-Midst: the Word becomes a child' by J. B. Jeyaraj from Indian and Asian contexts.

The key biblical narrative which forms the basis of the Child-in-the-midst method is in Matthew 18:1-10 (Mark 9:33-37; Luke 9:46-48) that depicts Jesus' act of placing the child in the midst of his disciples to show the disciples the way to the Kingdom of God. Furthermore, different terms have been employed by Child theologians that directly mean or imply agency. They are 'agents', 'lens', 'views', 'impact of the child' and 'active participants.'[46] However, the contentious thought that Child theologians present is that this act of Jesus is not *about* children in their context or the understanding of their development, "but to understand fully what children reveal to us of God and his purposes and nature."[47] They say again that children are partners in God's mission, the child and childhood are God's way of seeing all humans, children are messiahs,

[46] Collier, *Toddling to the Kingdom: Child Theology at Work in the Church* (London: Child Theology Movement, 2009), 19.

[47] Keith White, "The Child in the Midst of the Biblical Witness" in *Toddling to the Kingdom: Child Theology at Work in the Church,* ed. John Collier (London: Child Theology Movement, 2009), 156.

and children are representatives of Jesus and his Kingdom.[48] These biblical notions about children offer us both the symbolic significance of children, which has the possibility of remaining a restricted and controlled symbol in the adult discourse, and a strong theological basis to build the biblical theology of childhood and the agency of the child. However, what perhaps holds back the strong advancing of the agency of the child is White's way of seeing it: "to see the child in relation to God in Jesus Christ."[49] The children in our midst are seen in reference to God or Jesus Christ, and not as meaning makers by themselves.

There is an ambiguous relationship between children as symbolic presence in our immediate contexts and children as actual theological signifiers. However, the explanation for the agency of the child in the liberationist discourse must include their actual presence that will consider children's views and expressions. The following are critical exploration of the Child-in-the-midst method.

The Child-in-the-Midst: A Symbolic and a Silent Presence

For Child theologians, the presence of children or their absence does not seem to be of hermeneutical significance as the theologians seem to read the act of Jesus purely symbolically and at times literally. On the physical presence of a child, the child theologians explain that the mention of children is not necessarily about their physical presence. Therefore, a crucial question here is: What is the kind of a child envisioned in this method? John Collier says, "It should not affect us whether or not children are actually present."[50] White and Willmer consider the child in the biblical passage as a symbolic child or a child pictured in our minds as perceived from our contexts. They further establish this restricted symbolic idea by a literal reading of the act of Jesus the child that is placed in the midst of the disciples is a silent child, yet it stands in "splendid isolation." And, "[a] child should influence the way we do theology … It might be

---

[48] White, "The Child in the Midst", 157-160.

[49] White, "The Child in the Midst", 156.

[50] Collier, *Toddling,* 11.

to plant a mustard seed in one child or to allow a child to plant one seed in me."[51] Again in White and Willmer's words:

> The child is like a lens through which some aspects of God and his revelation can be seen more clearly ... the child is like a light that throws existing theology into new relief.[52]

They say again that the Child-in-the-midst is like a sacrament, as a visible word. When Jesus placed a child in the midst, it was more than a liturgical routine: it was a crisis of conversion, a shaking argument.[53] The above interpretation strongly suggests adult-advocacy over against the agency of the child as Jesus and his disciples engage in a conversation *about* the child.

White and Willmer's thoughts take obscure positions on the place of the child. While they mention that a child's silent yet physical presence is good enough to 'throw light' on the Kingdom of God and to trigger new insights for a radical theological argument, there also mention of the child as 'planting a seed', the child as a 'lens', and the 'child as a sacrament' offering a picture of an actively participating child. While White's presentation of the child as sacrament and lens tend to depict a positive view about children, they however suggest to underplay the views or perspectives of children as primary theological and methodological criteria.

Giving the whole argument a Christological turn, White mentions that the revelation of God or God's kingdom through a child cannot be on par with the revelation of Jesus. While this statement stands the traditional doctrinal ground, what has to be noticed here is White's succinct theological fear that the agency of the child would either eclipse or sideline God in Jesus. White says,

> However precious any part of creation is (and children are very dear to God's heart) anything that displaces God will tend to become an idol and in relating to any such

---

[51] Keith J. White, *Introducing Child Theology: Theological Foundations for Holistic Child Development, Revised Edition* (Penang, Malaysia: MBTS, 2010), 14.

[52] White and Willmer, "Our Response" in *Toddling*, 6.

[53] White and Willmer, "Our Response", 20.

> created thing we will tend to become guilty of idolatry however indirectly and unconsciously. So I would like to stress that all of us must take good care never to think or act in a way that elevates children or childhood in such a way that God is relegated to the background.[54]

While expressing his fear, White does not see that he subtly reinstates the adult-child binary through a bigger God-human binary where the adults usually represent the humanity when he says,

> It is necessary to emphasise that the child should not be the primary focus of criterion in Child Theology, because the child is not God. There is a danger of inadvertent or practical idolisation of the children, so that in child-friendly religious discourse the child in effect takes the place of God. Then, rather than the child being upheld and justified by the truth of God, the child would subvert and block the truth of God and our thinking for children would be deprived of the help of God.[55]

White explains again that Child theology as explained by its method respects the "experience and the voice of the subject by letting the child speak" but would not consider it evidential for the agency of the child.[56] While White's words show awareness that the agency of the child is effective in re-understanding theologies, the real voices of or the presence of children, the crucial constitutive elements of the agency of the child, is not very significantly advanced in the explanation of the method.

What White does not seem to have considered in his argument is the prevalent adult-child binary. Rather, he works within a divine-human binary. White depicts the elevation of the agency or the spoken words of the child as a direct contest to the agency of the divine. He does not recognize that elevating the agency of a child is to contest the dominant agency of the adult and not to replace God

---

[54] White, "The Child in the Midst", 154.

[55] White and Willmer, "Our Response", 21.

[56] Grobbelaar, *Child Theology*, 9.

or Jesus Christ. This contravenes the broader discursive framework of Child theology, which is basically to challenge adult-centric views. With this, White indirectly reinforces adult-dominance in Child theologies.

Furthermore, White proposes an argument that individuality of children advances the agency of the child over against communities of children in contexts. Can an individual child represent children in varying contexts of privileges and deprivations? For White, understanding children as communities would equate them to the marginalised adults who develop resistance in context of the violation of their agency. Therefore attending to children's issues individually would help to carefully discern their limitations and the scope of their agency. He says,

> Each child should be called and helped to be the agent of her own history, to be and become a particular person, but that development is prevented or distorted if children are treated as a group, a new type or generation of humanity which will transform the world...[57]

White stops short of explaining why treating children as group inhibits children's agency. Combining his views on not allowing children's voices to get prominence, the need for a God-human binary that reinstates adult-dominance, to address the needs of a child individually and not to equate the community of children to the community of the marginalized adults because they cause a revolution suggests in White a strong tendency to retain the power conventionally in the adult and to subtly overwhelm any notion of opposition or resistance from children.

The Child-in-the-Midst: Contextual Experiences of Children

A significantly contrasting interpretation to a silent or symbolic child is presented by Jan Grobbelaar who considers as significant the actual children in African context and the violation of their rights.

---

[57] Keith White, "Thinking about Child Theology in the context of Liberation Theologies" (paper presented at the Oxford Centre for Mission Studies, Oxford, November 30, 2010).

Grobbelaar raises an important hermeneutical question: "Who is the child in the midst?... Who are the children we put into our midst in our theological reflections in the twenty-first century... ?"[58] He answers these questions on the lines of Child theology in the west, however with a twist. To say it differently, Child theology seeks new knowledge and understanding of God's ways by living with children the way God desires.[59] It becomes crucial for Grobbelaar that "the child had no status in the surrounding Mediterranean world."[60] The child in the midst denoted marginalization and powerlessness.[61] If the child is not without a context, Grobbelaar fears that Child theology would become a "theology-from-above", and not any more a "theology-from-beneath."[62] He also adds that that children have their own spiritual experiences and "they are equipped with the Holy Spirit to bear fruit and to practice the gifts they receive from the Spirit. Although not regularly or universally applied, the agency of the child is not a new idea for the African mind.[63] Grobbelaar appeals to biblical insights on children's agency to confirm the practical experiences of children.

In his explanation of a contextual understanding of the child-in-the-midst method, Grobbelaar focuses on children who are always in a context and in a group with other children.[64] Grobbelaar, however provides ambivalent positions on what could constitute the agency of the child. Adults could imagine children in their context and reformulate theological ideas that accept children in the midst.[65] He emphasizes on the context of the children and places the onus on the adults to interpret the contextual lives of the children. He

[58] Jan Grobbelaar, *Child Theology and the African Context,* (London: Child Theology Movement ltd: 2012), 19.

[59] He employs a "reading with" posture as suggested by Gerald West, and therefore tries to develop a concept "reading with children". Grobbelaar, *Child Theology,* 18, 22.

[60] Grobbelaar, *Child Theology,* 19.

[61] Grobbelaar, *Child Theology,* 20.

[62] Grobbelaar, *Child Theology,* 21.

[63] Grobbelaar, *Child Theology,* 84.

[64] Grobbelaar, *Child Theology,* 39.

[65] Grobbelaar, *Child Theology,* 22.

however, more plainly, acknowledges that children have their own agency and it enriches the broader view of life as well as their own and their future. It can be noticed that Grobbelaar is flexible in appropriating the broader objective of Child theology to a local method, thus adapting methods from both the theological and the contextual ends. He presents the method in ways that could draw from the experiences of children in specific contexts, especially through children's own expressions of their experience. Unlike White, he does not rule out the possibility of children's own views as having agentic significance. What is also significant in Grobbelaar is the bearing that community has on a group of children and not just an individual. While White's symbolic or silent child represents the adult domain of God, Christ and theology, Grobbelaar's 'children as a group' helps bring out children's best agency in the midst of their peers and from their lived experiences.

The Child-in-the-Midst: The Word Becomes a Child

A sociological reading of Incarnation by Jesudason Jeyaraj revisits the child-in-the-midst as an Incarnation theology *from below*. Jeyaraj proposes the *from below* incarnation of Jesus as the starting point for Child theology:

> Jesus, the incarnated child, was at risk at the time of his birth and sought by the political authorities. The incarnation of Jesus in the midst of people reminds us of the weak, dependent and powerless nature of children and becomes the hope of salvation.[66]

For Jeyaraj, *logos* Christology is not just about power but also about frailty and vulnerability. He emphasizes two level of Jesus' earthly life:[67] *first,* Jesus the child was placed in the midst of socio-political risk; and *second,* Jesus as an adult, whose childhood and the understanding of children around him, molded his life and

---

[66] J. B. Jeyaraj, "Child in the Midst: Incarnation and Child Theology." In *Children at Risk: Issues and Challenges,* edited by Jesudason Jeyaraj, (Bangalore: Christian Forum for Child Development/ISPCK, 2009), 70.

[67] Jeyaraj, "Child in the Midst", 54-68.

teachings. At the first level, Jeyaraj takes the attention away from the love of the Father to give his only son to the world who becomes a human to dwell in a historical context. The limitation of *logos* is that it is both the Father and the son. But the *logos* that becomes flesh emphasizes human frailty and vulnerability. Jesus' dependence on parents, his neighbours and the socio-political contexts shows the societal influence on this grooming. Taking this aspect further, Jeyaraj says:

> [The] significance of his dwelling among human beings can know God through his words and actions. His dwelling among the people ... signifies his presence and identity with human beings.[68]

Incarnation from below gives hope to Child theology because Jesus went through a stigmatized life as an illegal child, yet Jesus' thoughts and words brought salvation. Such a Jesus would be able to identify himself with children.[69] Jeyaraj's contribution to the discussion on Child theology is to highlight historical semblances between Christ as an incarnate child and the conditions of vulnerable children in our midst. While Jeyaraj attempts to emphasize the humanity of Jesus through sociological readings, yet he connects the life of Jesus back to what he had tried to move away from, divinity. However, he evidently wants to retain the sociological aspect of Jesus life. He mentions that while the divine benefits of grace and salvation of God through the incarnate son

> cannot be taken for granted... [h]is incarnation among human beings is sociological in terms of his birth, growth, presence, relationship and consequences... [Therefore] Child theology is not only theological but also *sociological.*[70]

The second level of Jeyaraj's presentation of the human Jesus is the adult Jesus' act of recognizing the agency of the child in his

---

[68] Jeyaraj, "Child in the Midst", 58.

[69] J. B. Jeyaraj, interview by researcher, Madurai, India, March 16/17.

[70] Jeyaraj, "Child in the Midst", 59.

ministry. When Jesus places a child in the midst of his disciples he was presenting children as signs to the kingdom. He was also warning his disciples (adults) not to be stumbling blocks to children. The danger of orienting children to an adult life is to overlook the limitations of the adult life. He calls for an interaction between childhood and adulthood where childhood is more recognized than earlier and where the childhood as a significant stage in itself is acknowledged. In a sense, Jesus was carrying out a ministry by incorporating the significance of children that he was not taught about.[71] Thus, he clearly places children in historical contexts and invites contextual challenges in the hermeneutical schemes of Holistic Child Development.

Yet, a vital question that begs an argumentative response is 'what is the role of the child in its own liberation'? In answering this question lies the attempt to redefine the agency of the child within the context of liberation theology. Conversely, when theologies are adult activities, where do children's voices fit in? Are children's views taken as they are or modified to fit into the language of an existing theological thought? How much are children allowed to express their views as candidly as they could? A constant ambiguity that is evident in the above commentaries is 'what is more important in the child-in-the-midst method': the active presence and agency of the child or the solidarity of the adult in the best interest of children. As a progressive step, the child-in-the-midst method draws on the biblical model of Jesus placing the child in the midst of the adult disciples to whom the child becomes a model to enter the kingdom of God. The presence of a child seems to be central to the narrative. Furthermore, the child-focussed theologies have also been presented as creative theologies drawing from explanations that the agency of the child emerges from childhood as a stage in itself. The African contextual version of Child theology strongly proposes children's own views as theologically and methodologically significant in pursuing the agency of the child. It draws its theological strength by methodologically drawing from the positives of liberation theologies that endorse the views of the marginalized as either a

[71] Jeyaraj, "Child in the Midst". 59.

counter discourse or a critical continuum of the previous 'dominant' discourses.

Alongside the progressive strides that Child theology has shown, as a step backward, the children that are placed in the midst of the adults are expected to be passive and silent. It was noticed that a literalist reading of the child-in-the-midst passage in the Bible will block advancing the agency of the child by expecting silent and passive children around us. Understandably, the primary attention is given first to safeguarding the rights and dignity of children which is an adult activity. Even where there have been optimistic explanations for a positive agency of the child, a strong theological argument for the governance of adults over children is still prevalent.

Theological and Methodological Development of Children-Related Theologies in Asia: Insights from Historical Trajectories

As a matter of recognising some crucial sparks of children and theology which will otherwise be unspoken about, there was an emergence of and discussions on "children theology" (*Kulandai Iraiyal* in tamil) in India in 1990, much before the emergence of Child Theology Movement outside Asia. *Kulandai Iraiyal* was discussed by Israel Selvanayagam. Selvanayagam also recognised the adult-child binary and more importantly the lack of children's agency in Christian thought.[72] The child-focussed theologies like Child theology in the west and Asia and Holistic Child Development began around the year 2002. The Children theology in India recognised children's own views as significantly defining the agency of the child that largely emerge from children's context and children's interaction with adults. Children theology proposed a contextual understanding of children which is different from Child

[72] *Kulandai Iraiyal* or Children theology as a discussion was published in Indian local language Tamil in the journal *Iraiyiyal Malar* in 1990. While it did not continue as a prominent thought as the present Child Theology movement, it can certainly be said that the objectives of the present Child Theology Movement were discussed in *Kulandai Iraiyiyal.* These discussions took further shape in 1995 in Israel Selvanayagam's, "Children Laugh and Cry: Authentic resources for Christian Theology, *Asia Journal of Theology,* vol. 9:2 1995: 352-366 .

theology's less emphasis on context. However, children's theology neither developed into a deeper theological discourse nor associated itself with theological streams that propagated the agency of the colonised or marginalized children like the liberation theologies in India and elsewhere did.

Among the streams that strongly emerged in various parts of the world, a narrow sense of provincialism and confessionalism has restricted advancing of a deeper sense of agency of the child. This has drastically restricted the scope of the understanding of the agency of the child in the bigger discourse. The relationship between Holistic Child Development and Child theologies in the west is largely to address the place and significance of children in the light of the violation of their rights and dignity and to advance their agency. Holistic Child Development and Child theologies have a few things in common. They both help the church and community "to help children to serve children better."[73] However the differences are stark when Holistic Child Development has children at the centre of its theological thought and action while Child theologies "will have Jesus Christ at its heart."[74] However, White explains that the primacy of Christ is not at the expense of children because Jesus himself gave children a central place for them to thrive.[75]

However, the relationship is problematic and it could be analysed at two levels: [a] their interactions at conceptual levels project a subtle need for dominance over the other, and [b] identifying their commonalities and differences in the child-in-the-midst method. While this chapter explains in detail the commonalities and differences in the child-in-the-midst method, the interactions at the conceptual level between Holistic Child development and Child theologies in the west provides us evidence for a quietly dominant-natured Child theologies in the west in its interaction with its Asian counterparts. This highlights that Child theologies in the west have a strong colonial sense of imposing its methodological schemes on other child-focussed theologies. Even

[73] White, "Come over to Macedonia", 181.

[74] White, "Come over to Macedonia", 181.

[75] White, "'Come over to Macedonia", 181.

Holistic Child Development in the thoughts of Jeyaraj tries to claim its superiority over Child theologies. However, White continues to subtly present Child theologies as a superior stream among the child-focussed theologies.

To explain my contentions briefly, Holistic Child Development and Child theologies in the west emerged around the same time in two different geographical regions and contextual circumstances. However, Child theologies contend to offer "a long term paradigmatic shift."[76]

Keith White prepotently claimed that Child theologies have hermeneutical principles *to offer* to Holistic Child Development. However, he does envision beneficial learning for Child theologies from Holistic Child Development. He says that Child theologies have "no desire to dominate or control"[77] but hope to offer Christian "theological foundations" which it thinks Holistic Child Development lacks. With this he goes on to emphasise the primacy of Christian foundation as expressed in Child theology for Holistic Child Development against any developmental theories.[78] Even in his more recent work,[79] White continues his strong critique of the Holistic Child Development by presenting it as secondary to Child theologies. While engaging James E. Loder's ideas of human development, particularly children's development with Child theology, White sees a need for "connections" for an integrated approach. However, White sees Loder's ideas only "challenging" Holistic Child Development and not offering connections for integration. If Loder is a reference to a superior theological argument in human development, then Child theologies, for White, have reached a stage of conceptually engaging with Loder while Holistic Child Development is "still looking for some sort of synthesis, rather than accepting inherent contradictions between the different

---

[76] White, "The Contribution of CT", 1.

[77] White, "The Contribution of CT", 16.

[78] White, "The Contribution of CT", 16 pp.

[79] Keith J. White, "Child Theology, Loder, and Holistic Child Development (HCD): 50ff. This dominant position can be also be seen in his "Come over to Macedonia", 178-187.

discourses that make up for the components of an integrated approach."[80] As if it is not enough of a critique, White resorts to what would certainly be a harsh theological jibe to undermine Holistic Child Development when he says,

> Jesus confronts HCD in and through the sign of the little child with a dramatic challenge to change. He calls us to consider that we might be fundamentally mistaken, or on the wrong track—i.e., not just that we have made one or two minor errors, or slipped up occasionally, but that we are heading in completely the wrong direction. Of course we find it unthinkable that we might be outside the kingdom of God and getting further away in our striving for greatness in it! But hopefully we can see that there is a real practical problem here about process: the way any form of conceptual integration might be achieved.[81]

It is this position of White that ascribes to Child theologies conceptual superiority similar to colonial intellectual domination, and disables it from engaging with other child-focussed theologies. One can also notice Jeyaraj prompting a methodological argument on the relevant form of child-focussed theology even as Holistic Child Development and Child theologies exhibit methodological acquiescence at various levels. He explains why Holistic Child Development should be an "umbrella" concept to the wider field of child-focussed theologies. On the relationship between theological proposals emerging from Child theologies in the west and Holistic Child Development, Jeyaraj is clear that "Holistic Child Development is the over-arching umbrella or goal for which Child theology provides a theological basis for actions."[82] He claims that Child theology is fundamentally "biblical" and that Holistic Child Development is the "ultimate goal of this theology … They are integrated as theology and praxis

---

[80] White, "Child Theology", 51.

[81] White, "Child Theology", 51.

[82] Jeyaraj, "Child in the Midst: Incarnation and Child Theology." In *Children at Risk: Issues and Challenges,* edited by Jesudason Jeyaraj, page nos. Bangalore: Christian Forum for Child Development/ISPCK, 2009), 71.

and should not be separated."[83] The objectives and directions of the Holistic Child Development keep themselves open to engaging with Child theologies while Child theologies try to overlay theological principles and directives.

It can be noticed that the explanations for the child-focussed theologies as liberation theologies are ambiguous and show a less committed stance to advance the agency of the child. The much sought after preferential-option argument on behalf of children has been found inadequate. More precisely, there is a distinguishable struggle between the symbolic and the actual child. Furthermore, there is an emphasis on the contextuality of the interpretation rather than on the agency of the child. These accounts lack deeper exploration of liberationist principles such as the agency of the child as the preferential option and the rooted solidarity of the adult community. Significantly, a theological argument about the place of God and Jesus Christ alongside the agency and the solidarity has to be affirmingly established.

[83] Jeyaraj, "Child in the midst", 71.

Chapter 3

Challenges of the Agency of the Child to Christology

The debates on the agency of the child poses searching questions to traditional streams of theologies. This chapter addresses some challenges of seeing children's agency as a key to questioning and enhancing the scope of Christology. To reiterate, the term agency is used in the sense of including self-present consciousness of children that facilitates their views and expressions. It explains the ways children are able to stand out of the traditional normative moulds assigned to them through their actions, thoughts and behaviours. At times the thoughts and actions of children reflect the normative society, yet offer subversive opinions, if the adult-world keenly paid attention to them. In that sense, children are central to and crucial in offering unexplored trajectories in Christological engagement.

The key argument here is that an in-depth and systematic understanding of the agency of the child and childhood is essential in the ongoing process of reconstruing and reconstructing Christology. The argument further explores ethical and theological exercises we have shied away from in deconstructing these adult-child binaries at christological levels. Therefore, the debate moves beyond just the deconstruction of the binary to observe subtle expressions at the intersections of Christology, solidarity and the agency of the child in biblical and theological debates.

The child-in-the-midst method of Child theology and Holistic Child Development affirms the agency of the child based on the biblical mandate that Jesus placed a child in the midst of the disciples, emphatically opening up the agency of the child to show the way to the kingdom of God. The method then means using the lens of children to revisit our theologies and doctrines. My contention is that the child-in-the-midst method—despite offering strong liberative principles to see children as agents of theological discourse—sometimes subtly or explicitly—continues to safeguard an adult-Christological bias. As if that is not a drawback enough, another compelling contention is that the method does not debate Jesus' own adult-biases against children and how that could affect our Christologies. Therefore, we are yet to rethink a strong child-liberative Christology. In this line of thought, the chapter attempts to uncover the adult-child binary at various levels of the method by exposing the adult craving for didactic dominance and theological competency by safeguarding the potential adultism[84] in Jesus.

To explain this mode of adult-christological bias, there has been a thought among Child theologians that any discussion that advances the centrality of children means the danger of displacing Jesus Christ's sole centrality in our faith and practice. It would even be a sacrilegious act.[85] A similar apprehension has been expressed by DJ Konz in his proposal for a child-attentive methodology because

[84] Adultism means adult perspectives and prejudices dominating children's discourses in various contexts. It is an uncritical judgement about children by the adults due to their cultural entitlement of being considered powerful. In the words of John Wall, it is a historically sustained and "ingrained biases in favor of people who think of themselves as adults". John Wall, *Children's Rights: Today's Global Challenge* (Rowman & Littlefield Publishers, 2016), 3.

[85] Keith White, "The Child in the Midst of the Biblical Witness" in *Toddling to the Kingdom: Child Theology at Work in the Church,* ed. John Collier (London: Child Theology Movement, 2009), 154.

terms such as child-centred or child-centric and their methodological directions "risk displacing God as the primary object of theology."[86]

A significant realm of theological analysis which has not been strongly projected is the adulthood of Jesus and how audlthood as a culturally-entitled status could have had the adult-bias in his exhortations about children. This does not undermine Jesus' radically progressive teachings on the centrality of the child. Adrian Thatcher, in his understanding of Theologies of Childhood, rightly reiterates that "[i]t is necessary to prioritize the teaching of Jesus over against the rest of scripture..."[87] emphasising Jesus' proactive thoughts about children. While Thatcher's argument, in a sense, advances the agency of the child in the name of Christ, especially when many of our thoughts easily wander towards the passages that privilege the adults, his arguments are still found wanting on the adult-privileges that Jesus himself would have experienced in and through his thoughts and actions.

A child-inclusive Christology, instead of just focussing on the doctrinal divisions of divine-human binary, must recognize and integrate the interpretations emerging from the narratives of and around Jesus' life which is inclusive of childhood as much as adulthood. Our traditional mental images of and arguments for a liberative Christology are developed from the restricted imagination of Jesus as a grown-up adult and an always-preaching or telling-Jesus, a posture that signifies authority and control as an adult-entitlement. Even the theologies of Incarnation readily generate an adult Jesus because we read them through adult-lenses. Here, the analytical basis also involves some corrective understanding that Jesus as an adult could have had some adult-biases, yet constantly tried to overcome it by understanding children as central to God's new world order in a context of the empire that demeaned the place of children. While Jesus' location was one of dominant adult domain, he also presents a model of transformation from a default

---

[86] D. J. Konz, "Child Theology and its Theological Method, Past And Future," ANVIL: Journal of Theology and Mission Vol. 35/1: 25.

[87] As quoted by Jaan Grobbelaar in Jaan Grobbelaar and Gert Breed eds., *Theologies of Childhood and Children of Africa* (Durbanville: AOSIS, 2016), 136.

dominance mode to that of transformed solidarity. Jesus was a witness to the pain of children in the Greco-Roman period and also to the gospel emerging from children who went through pain, exposure and suffered as prisoners of wars and slavery. This is what Child theology overlooks in its biblical theology when it presents Jesus as using the lens of the child in pointing to the Kingdom of God. Jesus' exposition of the Kingdom of God comes from his critique of the Greco-Roman kingdom that dreadfully dealt with children coming from their colonies.

Christologies and Marginality of Children: Scrutinizing Apprehensions

Compelling the adults to re-read theologies through the lens of children is indeed path breaking. However, it has to be observed that the notions of the agency of the child will be hampered if the adults do not see their adult-privileges while wearing the lens of children. The progress of the theological discourse will be jeopardized if an exclusively adult Jesus is being employed as a reinforcement which will halt furthering the agency of the child. Our routine discussions on children focus so much on their victimhood *per se* that we overlook to critique adult entitlements. In this line of thought, there are various arguments in the child-focussed theologies through which the Jesus-child binary has been sustained. Sustenance of such binaries continues to privilege the adults in the name of safe guarding the centrality of Jesus. I will argue this through my reviews of the place of the child in the Christologies of the recent child-focussed theologies.

The adult-dominance is, in a sense, an annulment of the child-in-the-midst method. Biblically, the place of child in the midst of the disciples discusses a theological question in order to help us to be on the way to enter the Kingdom of God.

The Symbolic Child and the Misrepresented Jesus

A critical revisit of the child-in-the-midst method for a Christological viewpoint informs us that the presence of children or their absence does not seem to be of hermeneutical significance as child theologians read the act of Jesus placing the child in the midst of the disciples purely symbolically. Therefore, a crucial question here is: What is the kind of a child did Jesus envision in his act? As seen in the previous chapter, Child theologians do not look beyond the symbolic significance of Jesus when they say that it should not be of hermeneutical significance if the children are actually present or not.[88] The shift continues to centralise Jesus, whose speech about the child conveys the message of the Kingdom of God to his disciples. We continue to notice the struggle between projecting the children as significant beings and the cautious verbal confession to keep the children secondary to Jesus.

White and Willmer's thoughts on the sacramental significance of the child does not elevate the child to a real presence of the children in the sacramental life of a community. They mention that a child's inaudible yet actual presence is good enough to throw light on the Kingdom of God and to trigger new insights for a radical theological argument. The child presented here is a silenced child because of the powerful presence of Jesus. While White's presentation of the child as sacrament and physical presence tend to depict a positive view about the child, White and Willmer however suggest to underplay the views or perspectives of children as primary theological and methodological criterion.

The adult-child binary is strongly prevalent in our Christologies. Undergirding this presence is the human-divine binary where the adults represent the divine, and children are only a symbolic presence in the Christological equation. These Christological equations are scripturally and culturally handed down through reinforced interpretations of an adult-Christ and Christ's headship of the household. As mentioned in the previous chapter, there is a conscious depiction of the elevation of the agency or the spoken words of the child as a direct contest to the agency of the divine through Christ.

At least four limitations from the above thoughts should attract our critical thought process: a. children are not the primary focus; b. proposing the vocal agency of the child is idolatry; c. the

[88] Collier, *Toddling,* 11.

child is only a limited indicator to God or the works of God; and d. the patronizing sense of of adult-sympathy could be justified by resorting to the centrality of Jesus whose representatives are adults. Where there is an adult depiction of itself as the representative of God or Christ in a context of lesser-known humans as children, there prevails adult theological demagoguery.

The theological depictions and disagreements about the place and the centrality of the child begs a Ricoeurean question: are Child theologians intensifying what could be an allegorical nature of the depiction of the child into a transgressing forms of discourse beyond the desired signification to create the "the Wholly other?"[89] Adult-Christology has a subtle, and at times deliberate, reinstation of the adult-child dichotomy to adults' advantage by protecting and benefitting from a bigger God-human binary. The adults invariably represent the unseen God or Christ, the adult, and claim a legitimized authority on interpretations of scriptures, education and children. Such a representation instils in us an erroneous theological anxiety of the idolisation of children. Converting this idea into theological politics, the adult dominance effectively sabotages multiple ways in which Christ could communicate to us a child and through children.

Contrary to the thought of Jesus placing the child as a symbolic act, the historical context around Jesus' time confirms that Jesus' act could be more than just symbolic. This has been well-researched and published even before the emergence of the child-focussed theologies. There have been clearly strong propositions that Jesus considered actual communities of children from his and surrounding contexts while picking up a child and placing it in the midst of his disciples to demonstrate the significance of children and their expressions as compelling theological matter. An understanding of children in Greco-Roman culture and society explains these views.

John Eastburn Boswell, David Verner and Everett Ferguson among others offer to us well-researched insights about the plight and low estimation of children in Roman colonies around the first century. The primary identity of the children depended on

[89] As explained in John Dominic Crossan, *Cliffs of Fall: Paradox and Polyvalence in the Parables of Jesus* (Eugene: Wipf and Stock Publishers, 2008), 13.

the family or household to which they were born.[90] Intellectually, children were treated as lacking in reason and therefore adults-in-the-making that required training, which included physical battering.[91] The households followed the patriarchal norms that benefited the male children greatly. Many children were brought as prisoners of war and sold off as cheap labour in the slave market. There was also a heinous practice of the young girls being pushed into prostitution and sex-trade to breed more children as potential slaves.[92] This fuelled the vicious circle of girl-children exploitation as disposable creatures among Greeks and Romans.

Boswell in his article *Expositio* and *Oblatio*[93] explains the heartless practices about exposing children to strangers in public squares. He argues that exposing a child to risk was not the intention of the parents but to "offer the child up to the kindness of strangers, to the mercy of the gods, to public welfare, to a better fate (than the natal parent could offer), or simply to his [child's] chances... *Expositio* was an *alternative* to infanticide." While Boswell agrees that such exposed children were picked up for slavery and pushed into such harsher lives, he argues his case from a non-infanticide perspective. Therefore, it is morally better for parents to expose their children than to strangulate them. He cites instances where a child is abandoned in a basket on the water or a child born out of rape or incest is left aside on a road side.

At a more critical level, one can again notice the either/or options argued out from the perspective of the adults (parents) with

---

[90] David C. Verner, *The Household of God: The Social World of the Pastoral Epistles* (California: Scholars Press, 1983), 34.

[91] Plato states: "Of all the wild beasts, the child is the most intractable; for insofar as it, above all others, possesses a fount of reason that is as yet uncurbed, it is a treacherous, sly and most insolent creature. Wherefore the child must be strapped up, as it were, with many bridles" (Plato *Leg.*, 808D), cited by D. L. Stamps, "Children in Late Antiquity," *DNTB,* edited by Craig A. Evans and Stanley E. Porter (Downers Grove, IL: Inter-Varsity Press, 2000), 197.

[92] Everett Ferguson, *Backgrounds of Early Christianity* 2nd ed. (Grand Rapids, Michigan: William B. Eerdmans Publishing Company, 1993), 56.

[93] John Eastburn Boswell "Expositio and Oblatio: The Abandonment of Children and the Ancient and Medieval Family", *American Historical Review*, 89:10-33.

least attention to children-at-risk. These forms of arguments also bring to light the researches have been taking up for centuries purely from adult-eyes while sidelining the right of livelihood of children. Hence, it can be well-sensed that abandoning one's own children in the name of adult benevolence has been uncritically perpetuated for long in Biblical interpretative traditions. The Child theologians are either cautious or oblivious to the oppressed place of children during the times of Jesus that would have compelled Jesus to bring the debate on children back to the public square.

A New Way of Living with Children and Christological Explorations

Drawing some christological insights from the previous chapter, Grobbelaar's and Jeyaraj's contextual methods of analysis offer great promises to see Jesus as a child-friendly Christ who deliberately places actual children in the midst of the disciples to counter the adult-centric nature of discipleship. Grobbelaar's views also confirm that actual children in fact do not displace Christ; rather, they signify Jesus' advancement of the centrality of children. The same promises can be seen in Jeyaraj's sociological reading of Incarnation, Incarnational theology from below where the Word becomes a child in our context and the child reflects the Word effectively.

Challenges and Ways Forward for Children-centred Christology

In his outstanding work *The Mystery of the Child*, Martin Marty develops the notion of mystery as an outline to understanding the presence and significance of children in an adult-dominant world. The understanding of mystery in children is not just transcendental or deontological. It is to consider the "changing circumstances with their apparently limitless contingencies, experiences, and choices..."[94] Marty explains why the child should be treated as a mystery: "Treating the theme of mystery effectively can lessen the temptation of adults to see and sustain dominance and control over the child…"[95] Marty's caution to ward off adult dominance

[94] Martin Marty, *The Mystery of the Child* (Grand Rapids/Cambridge: William B. Eerdmans Publishing Company, 2007), 52-53.

[95] Marty, The Mystery, 60.

in the realms of mystery offers theological inklings to a children-friendly Christology. A child-friendly Christology needs a radical understanding of God or Christ or mystery that, on one hand embraces children and, on the other, critique the adult-biases. While literalists such as White and others do not treat the child as a problem, they keep the theological activity of Child theology as and within adult-domain. Such theologies tend to be concerned about the disciplining of the child, taking away the exploratory possibility of the mystery of the child or reining in the child-Christ in the adult-dominant narratives.

It becomes clear from the Christological propositions of the child-focussed theologies that there has largely been deliberate insistence on deontological obligations to Christology in a manner to sustain adult dominance, meaning the adults represent Christ best. Douglas Strum's explanation for why advancing the agency of the child is a compelling liberative task is noteworthy. For Strum, the adult-child discourse is supposedly the "last strongholds of domination, parallel to master- slave and male-female relationships of the past, and hence constitutes a final frontier for liberation theology."[96] On the other hand, there have been hopeful signs for ways forward in envisioning the significance of children and childhood in reinterpreting Christology. The Christological signposts for the agency of the child comes across powerfully from the traditional front: the theology of Incarnation. Here the deontological contours of Christology is pulled towards the ontological realm where positive deliberations of childhood is one the most basic necessities in understanding Christology. It is also in a sense the much-desired critical evaluation of adultism.

While it is imperative to sense these compelling shifts in Christology, more attempts have to be made to re-read Christology through the positive images of children in the scriptures to draw equity. The positive images should especially be those where the child speaks or has an opinion about an event: immediate, past

[96] Cited by Bonnie J. Miller-McLemore, "Children and Religion in the Public Square," 394.

or future. Or else our Christologies tilt again towards the adult-dominant side of the spectrum.

The critique of adult-centric Christology towards a children-friendly Christology should also explore and interrogate the adult-privileged views of the first century Palestinian Jesus. For instance, Jesus' thoughts on the daughter of Syrophoenician woman (Matthew 15:21-28). Feminist theologians have exposed how some uncritical liberationist principles have unwittingly retained the maleness of Jesus in our Christologies and that such Christologies harbour strong patriarchal attitudes.[97] Likewise, naive Christologies that draw a liberative picture of Jesus, yet see children only as symbolic actors subtly yet certainly retain adult dominance in our Christologies.

Children and Messianic Christologies

The imagery of a child plays an important part in messianic expectations. The prophet Isaiah announces about a future *child* of David's line who will be the hope of his people despite much suffering (7:14, 16; 9:16). The same prophet also describes this future in terms of an idyllic return to the childlike innocence of the Garden of Eden (11:8–9). The prophet Zechariah has a vision of the messianic era as a time of peace and joy when "the streets of the city shall be full of boys and girls playing in them" (Zec. 8:5).[98] It should be noted that male children received greater attention in both social and religious realm of the Hebrew society. Infant males received the sign of the covenant through circumcision (Gen. 17:10-14) and were expected to take up covenantal responsibilities. A bias against girl children needs to be noted here as the expected messiahs or, for that matter covenantal initiations, were largely through male children and expected only male messiahs. Overall, not seeing children as messiahs or potential messiahs is a restricted or adult-biased reading of the messianic narrative.

---

[97] Rosemary Radford Ruether, "Christology and Feminism: Can a Male Saviour Save Women?" in her *To change the World*, (Crossroad, New York 1981), 45-56.

[98] Joseph A.Grassi, "Child, Children,"..., 904-907.

In their eagerness to portray Jesus as questioning his Jewish traditions and offering a liberative outlook, the Child theologians and theologians from Holistic Child Development overlook the task of explaining Jesus' adult biases. Analysing Jesus' conformity to his cultural and religious teachings helps us contextualize his character for a deeper Christological analysis. We see how Jesus drastically grapples with and overcomes the notions of demeaning children on the one hand and placing the children in the midst of the adults to show the disciples the way to the kingdom on the other. Just as we critique the adult-privileged notions of Jesus, there need to be adult-dominant critiques of the theological themes such as the image of God, signs of the covenant, messiahs and the central actors in the new world order of God as well. The Christological management in our theological discourses need to be revisited for an expansive discourse where children find a sense a belonging and also where adultism must be probed for its cultural domination. Importantly, our Christologies need to reclaim the positive images of children in the scriptures and in our traditions. They make way to Christology where Jesus Christ stands alongside children without him having to fear a displacement.

Chapter 4

The Agency of the Marginalized and Indian Liberationist Theologies

This chapter discusses the understanding of the agency of the marginalized in liberation theologies in India, which is largely influenced by resistant form of liberationist principles including similar positions from postcolonialism. This discussion is with the purpose of analysing the relevance of the principles for issues and challenges surrounding the colonized and marginalized nature of children and childhood in theologies and social practices. The nature of the liberationist principles as postcolonial in liberation theologies in India is a contested issue. They are presented as 'post colonial', post-colonial, and postcolonial. In the liberationist theologies, there is a stronger commitment to hermeneutics of resistance and methodological exclusivism than to the understanding of committed advocacy from wider communities while working towards advancing the agency of the marginalized.

The claims for liberation theologies as postcolonial could be critically observed by: [a] an understanding that the exclusive agency of dalits, women and tribals work as a resistance to colonial forms of classical Indian theologies and develop a fresh understanding of the agency of the colonised in exclusive spaces; and [b] identifying that theoretical discussions on the methodologies take new when they are tested in specific contextual engagement between the colonisers and the colonised.

Problematizing the Postcolonial in Liberation Theologies in India

Postcolonialism in liberation theologies in India is largely treated in a historical sense where dalit theology, feminism and womanist theology and tribal theologies critique the earlier theologies that did not consider the agency of Dalits, women or tribals. In principle, the agency of the colonised is limited to acts of resistance and therefore less-engaging or conversational with previous "classical" Indian theologies. Therefore, their theological methodologies are 'counter' methodologies. George Oommen presents the emergence of liberation theologies, especially dalit theology, as a consequence of the post colonial struggles where the historically and culturally colonised communities attempted to claim their distinct identity. The claim for a distinct identity was in the face of homogenizing trends found in political and cultural colonisation.[99] Arvind Nirmal sees colonizing or conquering motives in what he calls "dominant" theological traditions and proposes an anti-colonial rationale for methodological exclusivity. He presents his notion of a counter theology in the language of conquest as in expansionist motifs of historical colonisation. Nirmal explains:

> This exclusivism is necessary because the tendency of all dominant tradition-cultural or theological is to accommodate, include assimilate and finally conquer others. Counter theologies or people theologies, therefore need to be on their guard and need to shut off the influences of the *dominant* theological tradition.[100]

Likewise, James Massey, a dalit theologian, identifies four historical colonial movements that have influenced theological thought in India: Aryan invasion, the Muslim invasion, the British colonization, and the post-independent India's upper-caste domination to colonize

[99] George Oommen, "The Emerging Dalit Theology."

[100] Arvind Nirmal, "Doing Theology," 141.

dalits as an intra-national dynamic in India. Massey analyses the four stages thus: The foremost stage is the defeat of dalits in the hands of the Aryans which through the course of time was authenticated and "internalized" through scriptural myths and narratives. The success story of Aryans was introduced through social order based on caste system which is stratification based on one's birth. Massey explains that the knowledge system of Aryan success could not be overcome even with powerful invasions to India by Muslims or the British or through the religions that they brought through colonization. Massey criticizes the Muslim and British colonization for strengthening the caste status quo. In post-independence India, he sees the country back in the hands of the upper-caste, "the original colonizers of the Dalits."[101] Massey puts caste-based discrimination alongside many historical invasions that India has experienced. Dalit theology and other liberation theologies have claimed that classical Indian theologies carried with it colonial notions of domination and acquisition. Nirmal's methodological exclusivism is an instance of blocking colonizing influences from outside of the 'pathos' experience of Dalits. The concerns of Nirmal and Massey were to identify various forms of historical and cultural colonial impositions that emerged in classical Indian theology. These concerns have effectively created resourceful spaces for the aspirations of the Dalits. While answering the question 'can agency stand alone without advocacy from wider communities?', one recognizes the need for advocacy, solidarity and deeper and wider analysis of theological themes such as God, Christ, church, community, salvation and so on.

Alongside Nirmal and Massey, Gabriele Dietrich too employs postcolonial principles to identify internal-colonies that are historically created. She recognises different levels of and simultaneous forms of colonisations manifesting in India and their continued influence on theological thought. They are cultural, economic, political and religious. According to Dietrich, "the situation is not uniform… [the understanding of colonisation] has

[101] James Massey, *Down Trodden: The Struggle of India's Dalits for Identity, Solidarity and Liberation* (Geneva: WCC, 1997), 27-28.

to do with a different positioning within the colonial history..."[102] Dietrich takes the concept of the postcolonial further by asking how we could "liberate internal colonies while fighting new external colonisation." She contends that one cannot hope to be post-colonial without taking on the offensive nature of neo-colonial implications. However, Dietrich takes the postcolonial discourse further than Nirmal, Massey and Oommen by drawing attention to the question of identity and difference as explained in postmodern and postcolonial discourses. Here, her focus is on the historical development of colonisation and the post-colonial response to it. Dietrich explains

> In order to create a post-colonial feminist theology, it is not sufficient to recognize the colonial character of our church history and to attempt to recover precolonial identities. It is also not enough to focus on post-modern, post-colonial acknowledgement of "difference". We have to simultaneously address the neo-colonial economic and cultural onslaught. Trying to go beyond colonialism required to address the problem that capitalism recreates colonies externally and internally.[103]

This highlights different ways in which postcolonial discourses have been employed in the liberation theologies so far. The different natures of postcolonial methods in the liberation theologies fundamentally means that the question of agency has been discussed in multiple ways to suggest that the methodologies contain in them a flexible configuration of the agency of the marginalised and advocacy of the others. As found in the works

[102] Gabriele Dietrich, "Why Should Postcolonial Feminist Theology Need to Relate to People's Movements?" *Asian Journal of Theology* 19/1 (April 2005): 167.

[103] Dietrich, "Why Should Postcolonial Feminist Theology," 174.

of Monica Melanchton[104] and Jayachitra Lalitha,[105] postcolonial inclusivity works at an initial or ground level to discern how cumulatively the motif of liberation could be worked out with broader or flexible objectives for an interactive and a flexible postcolony.

As an initial note, we observe some shifting notions in the understanding of the postcolonial in the liberation theologies. It moved from critiquing the classical Indian theologies to seeing colonial imprints in intra-national and intra-cultural discourses. However, in these shifting notions the role of agency is largely resistant in nature. A positive consequence of resistance means that it gives the theologically colonized a scope to recreate their histories and theologies.

A Critical Survey of Methodological Categories in Liberation Theologies in India

The following section is a critical survey of how the agency of the colonised in methodological exclusivism attempts to open to an engagement outside its methodological boundaries but falls back into the 'exclusivism' category to reinforce an exclusivist position.

Methodological Exclusivism in Liberation Theologies in India

A crucial debate on projecting and advancing the agency of the colonised within liberation theology in India emerged strongly with Nirmal's call for methodological exclusivism. Methodological exclusivism has two distinct roles: [i] it disconnects itself from previous methodological hermeneutics and establishes new hermeneutical keys to develop new methodologies drawing liberative

---

[104] Monica Melanchthon, "Bathsheba Reconsidered: Sexual Violation and After", *Gender, Religion und Kultur* (Stuttgart: Kohlhammer Verlag, 2010): 77-100; Monica Jyotsna Melanchthon, "Akkamahadevi and The Samaritan Woman: Paradigms of Resistance and Spirituality" in D. N. Premnath ed., *Border Crossings: Cross-Cultural Hermeneutics* (Maryknoll, Orbis Books: 2007): 35-54.

[105] Lalitha Jayachitra, "Jesus and Ambedkar: Exploring Common Loci for Dalit Theology and Dalit Movements" in *Dalit Theology in the Twenty-first Century,* ed., Sathianathan Clarke, Deenabandhu Manchala and Philip Vinod Peacock, (New Delhi: Oxford University Press, 2010), 121-136.

resources from within one's own identity category; and, [ii] the new methodologies are placed as counter-discourses to observe limitations and excesses in previous methodologies.

Nirmal, in his attempt to promote the exclusive agency of dalits, presents pathos or the oppressed experience of dalits as the formative factor of their agency. He insists that

> a Christian Dalit Theology will be produced by dalits. It will be based on their own dalit experiences, their own sufferings, their own aspirations and their own hope. It will narrate the story of their *pathos* and their protests against the socio- economic injustices they been subjected to throughout history. It will anticipate liberation, which is meaningful to them. It will represent a radical discontinuity with the classical Indian Christian Theology of the Brahminic tradition. [...] This also means that a Christian dalit theology will be a counter-theology. I submit that all people's theologies are essentially counter-theologies. In order that they should remain counter theologies, it is necessary that they are also exclusive in character. This will be a methodological exclusivism.[106]

For Nirmal, "pathos" or the inner most pain constitutes liberative agency. Nirmal indirectly acknowledges the significance of praxis but emphatically affirms that "*pathos* is prior to praxis." The preference to pathos is because it is their condition that leads dalits towards praxis including "knowing God" as a method of "doing theology."[107] Praxis prior to pathos could lead to a dangerous engagement with those having privileged experiences with colonising tendencies. Therefore, exclusive pathos experience of the dalits is the primary factor to define a postcolonial agency.

Nirmal also presents a faith-based dilemma in debating what should be the most compelling factor for the exclusive agency of the dalits. For Nirmal, Christian theological activity should not resemble a "separatist movement" in Christian theological

---

[106] Nirmal, "Towards a Christian Dalit Theology," 58-59.

[107] Nirmal, "Doing Theology", 141-142.

discourse [but which is] "continuous with and in dialogue with other theologies in the Christian world."[108] Therefore he struggles to present an unambiguous explanation on how to make dalit theological discourse a Christian discourse while returning to the question of the 'dalit':

> The Christian for this theology is exclusively the 'dalit'. What this exclusivism implies is the affirmation that the Triune god—the Father, the Son and the Holy Spirit—is on the side of the dalits and not of the non-dalits who are the oppressors. It is the common dalit experience of Christian dalits along with the other dalits that will shape a Christian dalit theology.[109]

Nirmal ambiguously invokes the Trinity to give dalit theology a Christian face. However, he emphasizes dalitness over against the Trinity to give dalit theology a dalit identity. Nirmal creates a binary of the oppressor-oppressed by claiming that the Trinity is only on the side of the oppressed. Therefore, he supplements a powerful Christian doctrine of the Trinity to assert an exclusivist position as the primary methodological position to advance the agency of the dalits.

The limitation of Nirmal's argument about the Trinity is that Nirmal does not provide a theological rationale to support his argument why the Trinity takes only the side of the oppressed. Rather, he uses the doctrine as a religious and psychological reinforcement to argue the case of the methodological exclusivism. Compressed delicately between the Christian theological engagement and cultural discourse, methodological exclusivism prefers to be strongly rooted within cultural discourses. The Christian theological basis, as explained in the explanation of the Trinity, is only secondary. Therefore, Nirmal's understanding of pathos leans towards a cultural pathos sustained by the Christian theological arguments.

---

[108] Nirmal, *Heuristic Explorations,* 26.

[109] Nirmal, "Towards a Christian Dalit Theology," 59.

Rajkumar offers a robust critique of Nirmal's restrained concept of pathos. For Rajkumar emphasizing just the cultural pathos takes the attention away from the majoritarian presence of dalits among Indian Christians. Rajkumar is right in projecting the majority notion of dalits among Indian Christians because this majority notion presents dalit theology as a mainstream discourse which otherwise could be overlooked for its exclusivist position. To continue Rajkumar's argument as more open-ended than Nirmal's, Rajkumar claims that praxis is more significant towards a final description of dalit agency. It is also important to highlight here that Rajkumar's notion of the majority dalit presence combined with praxis presents a novel scope for dalit-engagement with various liberative resources without forfeiting an account of the exclusive agency. Therefore, the exclusivity of agency produces lesser possibility of the agency of the marginalised.

Methodological exclusivists continue to exercise caution to the colonised-coloniser engagement. Historically, if the majoritary dalit presence connived with the primacy of pathos to generate a strong agency of the marginalised, the exclusive agency should have generated a strong liberative agency. It is now evident that exclusivist and resistant form of theologies have yielded lesser liberation than anticipated. In this argument, the primacy of praxis seems significant as praxis opens up to engaging spaces between the dalit colonised and the dominant communities as they have offered more liberative resources to retrieve and strengthen the agency of the colonised.

Clarke expects dalit theology to exhibit liberativeness by being inclusive "because of the interrelatedness of theological knowledge and the inclusive character of the Christian community."[110] He wishes to see any theology as offering "trajectories towards the universality of God and the inclusiveness of all human beings in the purpose of this one creator."[111] However, Clarke himself prioritizes methodological exclusivism over theological inclusivism. His rationale to retain methodological exclusivism and open-up spaces within it for a creative engagement is to reconstruct and present

[110] Clarke, "Dalit Theology," 22.

[111] Clarke, "Dalit Theology," 21.

"pain as the core of experiential knowing that must frame and fund Dalit theology."[112] In other words, when subjectivity is a product of a wider system, it should not subsume the core pathos experience of dalits. Clarke also exhibits a strong movement towards an exclusive position when he says:

> Other communities can participate in doing dalit theology but must recognize their respective distance and respectful relatedness to the distinctiveness of Dalit pain-pathos.[113]

Clarke reiterates Nirmal's argument but within the parameters of a dalit exclusivist position. Sebastian explains this hermeneutical movement as a cautious yet an anticipatory exploration for "interrelational" and "reconciliatory" methods. He raises this hermeneutical movement when he explains that Nirmal was committedly traversing between exclusivism and inclusivism to explore.

> the inter-relationship and interaction between Dalit theology and other forms of theologizing, as well as between Dalit and other communities, including those communities whose present 'status' was achieved, at least in part, through use and abuse of dalit peoples.[114]

It can be noticed that while agency of the colonised as a consequence of interrelationality is not entirely rejected, the core experiences of dalit pathos is treated as significant and unique to understanding dalit agency. While the purpose of interrelationality is to explore various modes of liberative agency beyond just the exclusive agency, Nirmal and Clarke restrict the cultural pathos and theological explanation of God predominantly on the side of the exclusivist agency. Even as they push the boundaries of methodological exclusivism to see

[112] Clarke, "Dalit Theology," 22.

[113] Clarke, "Dalit Theology," 22.

[114] J. Jayakiran Sebastian, "Creative Exploration: Arvind P. Nirmal's Ongoing Contribution to Christian Theology," *Bangalore Theological Forum,* XXXI/2 (December 1999): 48.

fewer colonial forms of inclusivism, they are cautious and at times aggressively exclusivists.

Methodological Exclusivism in Feminist Theologies

Feminist theologies in India principally subscribe to methodological exclusivism. They interrogate patriarchy-caste nexus within their specific context as well as in theologies, including signs of such colonies in dalit theology.[115] Feminists emphasize political and moral agency for activities of those women who find ways to affirm their identity against all odds. Metti Amirtham explains that theologies benefit from the agency of women through their pathos of hardships. In this context, agency constitutes "*empowerment* as manifested in assertion, critical consciousness, resistance and autonomy within the respective structures."[116] Built into Amirtham's framework of agency are two significant signposts: the particular experiences of women, and experiences of women unique to different contexts and structures. These signposts make the definition of agency fluid towards empowerment of any vulnerable group. The pathos of women increases the claim among women to "have control over her own life, body and environment."[117] Therefore, agency for Amirtham is a "sense of autonomy" intellectually and physically to interrogate deprivations and traditional "myths and notions" that restricts freedom.[118] When methodological exclusivism opens up context specific experiences of women, women theologians have used autobiographical methods as a theological methodology as a mode of agency. This is to put the multiple identities of a woman theologian, a feminist, and a dalit in a kaleidoscopic context and show how these identities create situations to explore or curb agency in a male-dominant, caste-based and religious academia. While multiple identities help overcome dichotomies and restrictions, they also marginalize one in a strong identity-centred theological

---

[115] Dietrich, "Why should Postcolonial Feminist Theology," 168.

[116] Metti Amirtham, *Women in India: Negotiating Body, Reclaiming Agency* (Delhi: ISPCK, 2011), 42.

[117] Amirtham, *Women in India,* 43.

[118] Amirtham, *Women in India,* 45-46.

politics. Therefore, highlighting one's marginality allows oneself to be a critical insider and also overcome narrow identity-political theologies.

Methodological Inclusivism in Liberation Theologies in India

This section highlights the heuristic of methodological inclusivism to show that the agency of the colonised in liberation theologies could open up conversations with potential authentic advocates through interfaith movements and through an interdisciplinary approach. However, because liberation theologies in India are strongly driven by caste identity discourses, the discussions on inclusivism are inhibited by dalit theological discourse. Therefore, inclusivism reinterpreted in the light of methodological exclusivism provides a strong methodological reference.

Methodological inclusivism contests the exclusivism position but is predominantly supportive of the spirit of exclusivism and pathos. If dalit pathos constitutes methodological exclusivism, then methodological inclusivism consists of differing experiences of oppression of non-dalits, both men and women, who strive to come together and offer solidarity with the oppressed dalits. The differing experiences of oppression are from communities that are deemed dominant from the perspective dalit pathos but who openly stand by dalit struggles to form stronger alliance to the oppressive caste and related power dynamics. Therefore, methodological inclusivism operates when dalits, tribals and oppressed women come together for an effective liberation of themselves.

Inclusivism through Interdisciplinarity

Methodological inclusivism as a thematic critique of methodological exclusivism is a strong sign of flexibility to define the agency of the marginalized. Methodological inclusivism was emphasized by first generation dalit theologians such as K. Wilson, Franklin Balasundaram and Abraham Ayrookuzhiel. What is significant in their presentation is the drawing of motifs of dialogue and the interdisciplinary nature of theologizing that existed in theological methodologies in India. Wilson and Balasundaram foresaw the impending danger of an excess of the pathos experience as a dominant criterion for theologizing while Ayrookuzhiel dwelt on the historical experience of interrelatedness of communities based on similar experiences of oppressions. They critiqued the dualistic and limited nature of exclusivism.[119] Explaining the methodological inclusivist position as a critique of methodological exclusivism, Oommen contends that an exclusivist theology would cease to be a Christian theology, and liberation has been achieved for non-dalits as well as dalits.[120] Ayrookuzhiel considers interrelatedness in methodologies as a significant part of the religious heritage of India. He proposes the methodology of interrelatedness to dalit theology which will open up theological and philosophical spaces as well as motivation for praxis to enhance the vision of liberation. With this Ayrookuzhiel sees a renaissance in the dominant hindu tradition just as it would offer wider scope to reconfigure liberative schemes. Explaining this for a dalit context, he expresses:

> Since Dalit tradition is historically bound up with the caste Hindu tradition it will not be easy to resist the pressure from inside. Here the dalits are asking for change as insiders. Given the political weightage of the dalit community in India it will be difficult for the caste Hindu to resist their demands. A process of change in this will be in the spirit of dialogues of religions.[121]

Anderson Jeremiah's proposal for a 'synergetic' method in the context of multiple methodological possibilities offers "collective

---

[119] For Ayrookuzhiel's methodological suggestions for Dalit theology, see Godwin Shiri, "Study of Religion: Ayrookuzhiel's Search for a New Approach in the Context of Dalit Theology," in *Religion and Society* 43, No. 3 (September 1998): 39-53.

[120] George Oommen, "The Emerging Dalit Theology: A Historical Appraisal." *Indian Church History Review*, Vol. XXXIV/1 June 2000: 19-37.

[121] Abraham Ayrookuzhiel, "Distinctive Characteristics of Folk Traditions. A Proposal for the Study of the Religious Heritage of the Dalits: Some Methodological Considerations," in *Religions of the Marginalized: Towards a Phenomenology and the Methodology of Study*, ed., Gnana Robinson (Bangalore/ Delhi: UTC/ISPCK, 1998), 1-17.

engagement of individuals which produces a significant effect at the end."[122] In his words, a synergetic method "transcends narrow preoccupations, thereby encompassing human life in its entirety,"[123] overcoming particular confines of religious or political or other forms of restricted categories. The focus then is on the centrality of human agency and not on supernatural, otherworldly occurrences or objects.[124] While Jeremiah adopts the conventional method of critiquing pre-liberation Indian Christian theology as coming from the "elite" and leaning excessively on Vedic religious philosophy, he equally critiques the essentialised Dalit Christian identity. Essentialised identity subsumes multiple identities that dalits live as a day-to-day drawing the best of possibilities from religions and cultures around them.[125] Therefore, Jeremiah rightly provides a strong critique of an inclusivist vision within methodological exclusivism because the agency of the colonised is advanced and strengthen in the wider interaction.

Inclusivism and Peoples' Movements

Indian liberation theologies have been effective through their association with people's movements. Coorilos directs Dalit God-talk at once to be strongly rooted in the scriptures and in people's movements. He sees the "logos" paradigm from the gospel of John as a model for theologies to associate themselves with people's movements. Similarly, Coorilos mentions that Dalit theology too has its future by "pitching its tent" among the homeless and the rights-deprived just as the embodied Logos "pitched its tent among

---

[122] Anderson H. M. Jeremiah, *Community and Worldview among Paraiyars of South India: 'Lived' Religion* (London: Bloosmbury Academic, 2013), 165.

[123] Jeremiah, *Community and Worldview*, 165.

[124] Jeremiah, *Community and Worldview,* 165.

[125] Anderson H. M. Jeremiah, "Exploring New Facets of Dalit Christology: Critical Interaction with J. D. Crossan's Portrayal of Historical Jesus," in *Dalit Theology in the Twenty-first Century. Discordant Voices, Discerning Pathways.* eds. Sathianathan Clarke, Deenabandhu Manchala and Philip Vinod Peacock (New Delhi: Oxford University Press, 2010), 151.

people."[126] This could provoke the "philosophical imagination, sociological imagination and poetic imagination"[127] of Dalit theology in the contexts of Nandigram, Plachimada, Moolampally and Narmada struggles.

Oommen explains that many of the caste-based issues were reduced to economic categories due to an increasing impact of secular dalit movements alongside Latin American liberation theological movement that depended on a secular movement as Marxism. Oommen explains:

> ... caste is now seen as the major socio-economic formative force in shaping and understanding the history of dalits. Moveover, the over-arching impact of Ambedkarism on all Dalits further seems to enhance the process of accepting caste as the sole source of the suffering of Dalits.[128]

Therefore, dalit theology deploys class-caste assemblage to give space for the identity of the working class from the lens of the caste-oppressed. A minority religion such as Christianity in India has ever felt the need to extend its theology into people's movements to identify itself in a larger national scenario as well as to contribute to nation building as its obligation both in pre-colonial and post-colonial India. As Wielenga explains this phenomenon,

> Christian nationalists like M. M. Thomas started to recognise that their dreams at the dawn of Independence had not come true. Interaction with social scientists and activists convinced them that a radical renewal would have to come in the course of people's awakening and organisation and struggles. From then onwards the focus shifts from 'development' and 'modernisation' to 'social

---

[126] Geevarghese Mor Coorilose, "Dalit Theology and its Future Course" in *Dalit Theology in the Twenty- first Century. Discordant Voices, Discerning Pathways.* eds. Sathianathan Clarke, Deenabandhu Manchala and Philip Vinod Peacock (New Delhi: Oxford University Press, 2010), 168.

[127] Geevarghese Mor Coorilose, "Dalit Theology and its Future Course", 168.

[128] Oommen, "The Emerging Dalit Theology," 67.

> liberation' and from 'nation' to 'people', meaning tribals, Dalits, women, peasants and workers getting organised in the struggle for their rights.[129]

More specifically for a dalit cause, a need for dalit representation in the national scenario was strongly felt since India became independent in 1947.[130] The views of Bhim Rao Ambedkar, a pioneering dalit intellectual and activist, prompts Indian theology to incorporate political ideology into dalit theology for two reasons: firstly, as a Christian minority to benefit from the liberative vision that is constitutionally granted; and secondly, to participate in people's movement to bring about dalit liberation beyond religious boundaries.[131] The constitutional reforms signified the political voice of the dalits. It can be observed that when liberation theologies like dalit theology attempt to be inclusive through people's movements, they are drawn into a hopefully quicker sense of liberation and also does not stop with the discourse of the victimhood of the colonised. Coorilose introduces the concept of mystery by invoking the biblical concept of Logos. For Coorilose, the understanding of mystery

---

[129] Bastiaan Wielenga, "Liberation Theology in Asia," in *The Cambridge Companion to Liberation Theology,* second edition, ed. by Christopher Rowland (Cambridge: Cambridge University Press, 2007), 67.

[130] For a strong sense of critique and undermining the dominant Hindu philosophical politics, see Kancha Illaiah, *Why I am not a Hindu: A Sudra Critique of Hindu Philoshopy, Culture and Political Economy* (Calcutta: Samya, 2005). For analysis of cultural factors surrounding caste discourse, see Manoranjan Mohanty, *Class, Caste and Gender,* 3rd reprint (New Delhi, SAGE, 2006); Ghanshyam Shah ed, *Dalit Identity Politics: Cultural Subordination and the Dalit Challenge,* Vol. 2 (New Delhi/ London: Sage Publications/Thousand Oaks: 2001); Gail Omvedt, *Caste, Land and Politics in Indian States* (New Delhi: Authors Guild Publication, 1982); Gail Omvedt, *Dalit Visions: The Anti- caste Movement and the Constitution of an Indian Identity* (Hyderabad: Orient Longman, 2006).

[131] Aravind P. Nirmal and V. Devasahayam eds, *Dr. B. R. Ambedkar: A Centenary Tribute* (Madras: Gurukul, 1991); Mohan P. Larbeer, *Ambedkar on Religion: A Liberative Perspective* (Madurai /Delhi: DRC/ISPCK, 2003). Some of the prominent dalit movements in post- Independent India are the Dravida Movement, Dalit Panthers, Dalit Sangarsha Samithi, the Dalit Sena, Bahujan Samaj party, etc. Caste based struggles have been internationalized to mobilize attention.

which is associated with people's movements helps the colonised draw liberative solidarity from various people's movements.

Inclusivism and Interfaith Matters

While there is a strong contention within its methodological purview to maintain an exclusive notion at a broader level, dalit theology exhibits inclusivism. This openness is well captured in Nirmal's efforts to see which identity should take priority—the Christian identity of dalits or dalit identity of a Christian. While Nirmal seems to be wary of the term 'Christian' as it might overshadow the pathos argument related to caste identity, his cautious approach would mean that he does acknowledge the kerygma of Trinity at the core of his theological formulation without permitting it to permeate the caste identity. The nature of such a stance, Wielenga clarifies, was culturally built into an aspiration for liberation and to be retained:

> What is specific about Asia, especially in contrast with Latin America, is the religio-cultural context. The overwhelming majority of the poor and oppressed in Asia are non-Christians, many of whom adhere to a wide variety of popular religious traditions which are more or less connected with the traditions of the great religions which have shaped dominant Asian cultures.[132]

This poses methodological challenges to understand the agency of the colonised. Having identified the need for Asian liberation theologies to see liberative 'connections' with neighboring religions, Wielenga presents a defence of Christian liberation theology. Elaborating his defence through Kappen's words, Wielenga invites an inclusive spirit of Christian identity among dalit theologians that has been well-attested. Dalit theologians have tried to see liberative elements of various religious traditions in India as complementing Christian understanding of divinity and liberation from the divine. Joseph Prabhakar Dayam retrieves the theological imagination in the discussions of the Divine Feminine among Dalit communities. He specifically discerns the power and *Koriaka* ("desire") of

[132] Wielenga quoting Sebastian Kappen, "Liberation Theology in Asia", 55.

Gonthelamma of the Malas in Andhra Pradesh to challenge male-dominant christologies and to re-formulate Christian theology into theo/alogies for an inclusive vision of Dalit community.[133] Dalit theology can authenticate its relevance by correlating with resources "even if they are not Christian" as they enhance a "Christian conception of God."[134]

Examining methodological inclusivism, we noticed that there has been a strong contention between the majoritarian identity of dalits in Christianity and the minority identity at the national scenario. A common denominator that strongly defines the agency of the colonised in these debates is the 'pathos' discourse from both Christian theological perspective and the cultural perspective. If pathos is the defining factor to establish the notion of the agency, it falls back largely on the exclusivist mode without amply considering the role of the authentic advocates or the theological themes of God or the divine that could be inclusive. Even the role of the advocates and the divine are absorbed into the primacy of pathos. Therefore the agency that transpires here is largely an exclusive agency, however not without heeding to the authentic advocating presence coming from the dominant theologies. But it does not sufficiently consider the potential of methodological engagement with the inclusivist streams yet.

As the following section explains, oppressive experiences in India are not just based on caste discrimination but also on gender and tribal discrimination. Therefore, dalit theologies insistence just on caste oppression as the source of agency restricts the constituent factors of agency and the scope of dalit theology as a representative liberation theology in India.

Praxis and Liberation Theologies in India

As we saw earlier, Nirmal clearly prioritises pathos (methodological exclusivism) over praxis. However, we observed in methodological

---

[133] Joseph Prabhakar Dayam, "*Gonthemma Korika:* Reimagining the Divine Feminine in Dalit Theo/alogy" in in *Dalit Theology in the Twenty-first Century.*, 137-149.

[134] Clarke, "Dalit Theology", 31.

inclusivism that the criterion to advance the agency of the colonised can cross the boundaries of the discourse of exclusivism which includes the methodology of praxis.

Before I engage further in the discussion on pathos-praxis relationship and its significance to the understanding of agency, I highlight what praxis means in the context of Indian liberation theology. Maria Arul Raja offers two significant insights on praxis in dalit theology in particular and liberation theology in general that complete the process of liberation. They are a) identifying liberative aspects and, b) furthering the liberative aspects through praxis in the light of the scriptures. A liberative aspect is incomplete unless translated into a liberative action.[135] While in both cases the victims' agency is significant, it is clear that agency of the marginalized alone will not yield liberation. Liberation theology in India owes it vision of praxis to at least two wide ranges of sources emerging nationally and internationally: a. To secular people's movements and grassroot action groups in unsettling the western colonial power in India; b. to the Latin American liberation theological emphasis on the nexus of faith and politics, church and base communities, and multi-faith forums and Christian theologies. By doing so, it was trying to spread the process of liberation of the dalits and other marginalized communities. Thus enhancing agency, praxis resists an alienating tendency in attempts to forge solidarity. It poses an explicit sign of threat to the absoluteness of the oppressor. Solidarity of the like-minded for liberation acts as catalysts for wider liberation. It is precisely this solidarity that the liberationists in India find lacking in the classical Indian theologies. As discussed in the previous chapter, Christian philosophical theologies have less impact on Indian society because of their minority status. Ethical and political debates "gravitate towards an increasing assertion of the majority culture."[136]

At a theological level, the philosophical frameworks that classical Indian theologies adopted either from eastern or western theological traditions were allegedly from the dominant philosophical

---

[135] Maria Arul Raja, "Living through Conflicts: The Spirit of Subaltern Resurgence", *Vidya Jothi Theological Review,* Vol. 65 (June 2001): 465-476.

[136] Dietrich, *A New Thing on Earth,* 130.

stream. Liberation theologians resort to this argument and add that theologies are not action-oriented enough to bring about changes among the colonised. As Clarke reiterates, earlier Indian Christian theologians were reluctant to reflect upon "Jesus' concrete praxis." A lack of placing human subjects in a context would deprive them as "conscious agent."[137] It was here that Indian liberation theologies felt the need to extend their theological activity into context-specific actions and movements. This enables identifying a larger national scenario as well as to contribute to nation building as its obligation both in pre-colonial and post-colonial India. This has contributed to the agency of the marginalized at two levels: a quantitative increase of voice thus making the voices of the marginalized heard more effectively; and drawing unexplored resources for agency to envision a faster liberation.

Praxis has challenged methodological exclusivism and methodological inclusivism by a deeper engagement with the agency of the colonised, the advocating responsibility of the former colonisers and the dialogical nature of the oppressed from different walks of life and not just from dalit backgrounds. As Bennett explains, "praxis is not just an ethical position of a theological argument, rather praxis *is* theology."[138] In that sense it is an action-oriented engagement by the oppressed; and, action-oriented engagement on behalf of and along with the oppressed by those sympathetic to the oppressed. Therefore it is an engagement of the oppressed and oppressor in context-specific movements with liberation as the highest objective.

Continuing on the methodological inclusivism arguments of Balasundaram, Wilson and Ayrookuzhiel, Rajkumar confirms this methodological premise by terming the inclusive approach to praxis as a significant signpost for a theoretical notion of agency in dalit theology:

---

[137] Sathianathan Clarke, "The Jesus of Nineteenth Century Indian Christian Theology" *Studies in World Christianity* Vol. 5/1: 32-46.

[138] Zoe Bennett, "'Action is the life of all': the Praxis-based Epistemology of Liberation Theology" *Cambridge Companion to Liberation Theology*, 2nd edition, ed. by, Christopher Rowland (Cambridge: Cambridge University Press, 2007), 39.

> The agency for this [dalit] liberation lay not only with the Dalits but was also dependent on partnerships with non-dalits and other like-minded groups. This makes it incumbent for us to understand that the envisaged praxis of Dalit theology is essentially a praxis of partnership.[139]

Engaging in this debate, Rajkumar raises a critical question about the relationship between the identity-specific discourse and praxis, albeit in a reverse order.[140] While in this section I discuss how praxis contributes to deepen the understanding of the above-mentioned engagement, Rufus enquires into the potential contribution of the identity-specific discourse in Indian liberation theologies to deepen the understanding of praxis. A point of convergence between my argument and that of Rufus is that exclusive identities as manifest in methodological exclusivism deter the advancement of the agency of the colonised. I see in praxis a fluid and negotiating relationship between methodological exclusivists and methodological inclusivists with a bigger objective of advancing the agency of the colonised. On the other hand, Rufus explains that dalit culture discloses a sense of engagement and negotiation if dalit religiosity remythologises its narratives with "existential pragmatism" which inevitably requires the primacy of community and solidarity and interdependency.[141]

In this section I deal with three models of praxis that are clearly articulated in Indian liberation theologies. They are Peniel Rajkumar's 'Praxis and Imagined Identity', Mathew Schmalz' 'Spatial Oppurtunism' and George Nalunnakkal's 'Organic Womanism.'[142]

---

[139] Rajkumar, *Dalit Theology and Dalit Liberation*, 177.

[140] Penieel [sic] Jesudason Rufus, "The Problem of 'Methodological Fidelity' in Identify-Specific Hermeneutics and the Pertinence of 'Ethological' Hermeneutics", *Bangalore Theological Forum* XXXVIII/I (June 2006): 120-144.

[141] Rufus, "The Problem of 'Methodological Fidelity'", 122-126.

[142] In this research, I use the term Womanism as used in Indian liberation theological context which has multiple origins. It is a critical awareness that feminist theologies and theories as proposed by feminist discourses in the west that have influenced Indian theologies do not encompass the experiences of women in particular cultural contexts. It also critiques other liberation theologies in India such as Dalit theology and Eco-theology for not articulating the specific caste based oppressions of women and of those women are the direct victims of

Rajkumar's proposal clearly contests the core of the "imagined identity" of praxis that largely agrees with a space created by the dominant. His thoughts question the basic premise of Indian Christianity that historically prevailed for solidarity which is highlighted by Schmalz. Rajkumar exposes the historical paradox which is the so-understood dominant are only minorities in Christianity in India and that praxis needs redefining in the light of the dalit-majority.

Rajkumar makes important observations on convergences and divergences in agency-praxis interaction with different castes and tribal communities. Understanding solidarity as praxis, he observes, has a fundamental flaw in the notion of the 'solidarity of the church with dalits'. The church in India is dalit by majority, and dalits continue to interact with other caste and tribal communities to reclaim their voices. In the process they call the church to participate in a collaborative effort for the liberation of dalits. The call for the church to be in solidarity with Dalits means that the dalits are imagined to be the minorities. It is this imagined definition of the church that has delineated what should be the platform for dalit-agency praxis. Therefore the imagined church could only represent what it is not through solidarity in praxis. This restricts a clearer strategy for a stronger dalit-praxis due to continued demonstration of dalit/non-dalit binary in a predominantly non-dalit operated praxis.[143] Here Rajkumar is clear that the binaries could be overcome by acknowledging that the church in India is of dalit majority and therefore their agency will in effect take care of praxis simultaneously by addressing dalit-christology. Two issues stand out in Rajkumar's analysis: firstly, dalit Christology's engagement with praxis would enhance the scope of Dalit agency. Secondly, Dalit Christology

ecological degradation. As I will explain later on, Womanism here considers as vital the agency of dalit and Adivasi women's movements that struggle for the issues of land that they are strongly connected to in their particular region. This explanation if different from that of Alice Walker's who originally proposed Womanism that critically interrogates racist and classist aspects of white feminism. Alice Walker, *In Search of Our Mothers' Garden: Womanist Prose* (San Diego: Harcourt Brace Jovanovich, 1983).

[143] Rajkumar, Dalit Theology and Dalit Liberation, 60.

or dalit praxis will not be adequate enough to pursue dalit agency effectively independently in a multirrelgious context.[144]

It should be observed that Rajkumar's discussion contributes largely to, but is not restricted to, the ways in which praxis facilitates Christian theology by revisiting dalit theology. However, the question of how a redefined Christology helps a minority Christian praxis in a largely multi-religious context where the dominant Hindu philosophy is still the largest factor of theologizing in public sphere remains. Feminist theologian Amirtham's theoretical notion of agency was worked out largely on the lines of methodological exclusivism, but at times transcended that mode into methodological inclusivism as reflected in praxis. She describes "action-oriented groups", education institutions, and media as catalyst agencies.[145] She explains that those who have participated in these groups have claimed that these groups have given them a new type of consciousness to come out of their insulated enclosures and social spaces, expressing their equality, freedom and dignity in relation to men. Besides, the elements of transformation among women include empowerment, self-confidence, socio-cultural and political consciousness and assertion of self- identity leading to agency.[146]

The model of spatial opportunism, as proposed by Mathew Schmalz, starts spiralling from a non-pathos position into a space of practical solidarity with pathos. It creates opportunities of praxis for dalit liberation, providing the place within which the dalit agency could be recreated. According to Schmalz, as much as marginalisation is based on the differences, it also provides opportunities to understand the dynamics of relationships between the colonised and the colonizers. The marginalised must seize this opportunity to momentarily refrain from resistance and cross-cultural boundaries to gain freedom.[147]

---

[144] Rajkumar, Dalit Theology and Dalit Liberation, 122.

[145] Amirtham, *Women in India,* 150-151.

[146] Amirtham, *Women in India,* 150.

[147] Mathew N. Schmalz, "Dalit Catholic Tactics of Marginality at a North Indian Mission", *History of Religions*, 44/3 (2005): 249-251.

As Schmalz points out, the agency in praxis emerges even without being a victim of oppression and therefore not sharing in the pathos of the marginalized. When two Christian mission agencies create geographical spaces for education, health and housing, it immediately converts into a discursive space for dalits in hindu and other religions who make use of the space.[148] This space collaborates liberative dynamics of the sympathy and pathos beyond religious boundaries. While there could be a limit on the exclusive agency of the marginalized for a liberative praxis to create an agency in a non-pathos space, Schmalz yet sees an opportune space—which was not available earlier for the marginalized—to re-tell their histories. These histories were earlier enmeshed in metanarratives of the times and spaces that received either marginal or no attention.

Schmalz also highlights the intriguing notions of a liberative praxis when the praxis is expected to be supported by Christian theology. Many of the stories and activities of the marginalized, especially of the dalits are "dismissed as uninteresting" because they appear neither "Indian nor Christian."[149] Both 'Indianness' and 'Christianness' of praxis are largely influenced by the religious and cultural language of the dominant that have not incorporated dalit and tribal spiritualties as equally significant. Therefore, spatial opportunism as praxis opens up subversive spaces for reclaiming histories and agencies of the marginalized. There is a possibility of the marginalized not getting the spatial opportunity completely for themselves. Spatial opportunism also provides the same practical solidarity for methodological exclusivism. This opportunism overrides any clear-cut methodology at micro-levels of interaction in that there is a sense of the postcolonial overview of prioritising any one methodology and at the same time clearly advancing the agency of the marginalized. Spatial opportunism presents a way of establishing a collaborative praxis that would both restrict and enhance methods of liberation.

However, a multireligious context presents a challenging perspective for praxis. A model of political consciousness that

---

[148] Schmalz, "Dalit Catholic Tactics", 222.

[149] Schmalz, "Dalit Catholic Tactics", 217.

enhances theological scope of agency is the model of Organic Womanism, a model of praxis. This model fills in for Christian theology for being unable to affect the context with its Christian-only approach to praxis. The model as proposed by George Nalunnakkal combines gender and interfaith concerns to define agency. Nalunnakkal explains how organic womanism as resource for understanding agency is triggered by a mass movement in Kerala (India) initiated by Adivasi Gothra Maha Sabha ('The Grand Assembly of Adivasis' [Adivasis means '*original inhabitants*' or tribals]) "where a representative from each Adivasi village (with gender parity) *take decisions for themselves.*" The Maha Sabha struck an alliance with Dalits in Kerala. The main source of Nalunnakkal's proposal is a people's movement led by a tribal woman "unlike other political movements... [which] represent a new political awakening." It was led by Dalits and adivasis themselves. While Nalunnakkal is conscious of the inclusive nature of feminism which includes men as advocates in liberative project unlike womanism, he still feels that womanism in India "need not be seen as an exclusive enterprise of women alone."[150]

For Nalunnakkal, organic womanism will be interested in retaining a certain sense of 'methodological exclusivism, which is required for an identity politics oriented discourse [...] The adjective 'organic' is engaged here to highlight the natural relationship that Dalit and Tribal women have with nature, which women of middle class and other section of the society do not possess at the same level and intensity.[151] The fact that the herald of the movement is an Adivasi woman, articulating issues of social justice and ecological balance through the forum of 'Adivasi Gothra Sabha' is of immense political significance. Nalunnkkal reckons that highlight exclusive agency of the adivasis, ramifications for shaping the future course of eco-feminist discourse in India.[152]

A crucial methodological point in Nalunnakkal's proposal is that he emphasizes methodological exclusivism as a conceptual

[150] Nalunnakkal, "Towards an Organic Womanism".

[151] Nalunnakkal, "Towards an Organic Womanism".

[152] Nalunnakkal, "Towards an Organic Womanism".

base. I explain Nalunnakkal here to highlight the nature of praxis that Indian theological scenario offers. In chapter 4, I engage with Nalunnakal further to show how praxis, which has the potential to create engaging spaces, when combined with methodological exclusivism reduces the possibilities of engagement at the grassroots, thus largely restricting the agency of the colonised in the Indian context.

A Critical Review of the Agency of the Colonised in Liberation Theologies in India

This chapter surveys how agency, solidarity and mystery interact with each other at various levels in the methodologies of liberation theologies. The Indian liberation theologies, in the course of their history have either hesitantly or openly accepted liberative resources that are available even in the so-understood 'dominant' as seen in intertextual readings using postmodern methods or contrapuntal methods. This trait is clearly and consciously promoted by theologians almost in the first instance of formulating a methodology for dalit theology. The flexibility of methodological boundaries has helped the liberation theologies to gain from interdisciplinary interaction. Therefore, this directive opens up to appreciate the theological capital any marginalized discourse could offer.

Liberative resources have come not only in the form of philosophical discussions, but also in the form of solidarity of many marginalised groups like women's movements, ecological concerns, and class struggles. The pathos experiences of these marginalised groups may vary in their nature in different contexts, but a shared pathos of being rejected or neglected forms a common denominator in attempts to confront a dominant ideology.

It has clearly emerged from the discussions that there would be a constant and creative tension in a situation where many liberative ideas merge. Only a context could order what could be a good configuration of liberative resources for that specific moment. Therefore, any act of homogenizing *pathos experience* would become too predictable to survive an onslaught of powerful ideologies such as caste-based colonisation found in Christian theologies. As their limitations, dalit theology and other forms of liberation theologies have many unaddressed forms of colonies, and such colonies might project at various times and spaces. On a positive note, the liberation theologies have partly kept themselves open to be influenced by various forms of theologies outside the boundaries of methodological exclusivism.

Different generations of liberation theologians have amply exhibited how many gaps within dalit and other theological thinking have been critically diagnosed and plugged in with what is deemed as relevant at that point in time. A consistent evaluation of theologies incorporating positive insights from various generations is also metaphoric for the need to take the views of younger generation as creatively crucial for an inclusive theology.

Dalit theology has amply exhibited how it has benefitted from movements and secular academic disciplines. Within theological discussion it has richly enhanced its argumentative base after drawing from various theological disciplines. Indian theological scenario has been highly interdisciplinary in that it has drawn from all possible resources to step up the momentum of liberation and wider participation.

As observed, the homogenizing tendency of liberationist theological stream under class, gender, anthropocentric and such categories continue to be some of the strong identity-specific factor influencing the discussion on the agency of the marginalised. I also explained that exclusivism has the tendency to homogenise various degrees of pathos experiences as well as compel the methodological inclusivism to prioritise the primacy of pathos. Homogeneity dangerously subsumes differences. Liberation theologies as in dalit theology have a history of and potential to homogenize struggles of different peoples-group.

Agency, Solidarity and Mystery

To explain the nature of agency that emerges from this discussion, methodological exclusivity presents an agency that stands independently from the potential advocacy that methodological inclusivism offers. While advocacy of the sympathetic marginalised is present with its liberative resources to strengthen the case of the pathos, methodological exclusivism presents strong resistance to such sympathetic presence by suspecting colonial traces in their presence. Therefore, when the theme of agency is emphasised, it is largely in an exclusive sense. When there are attempts to expand the understanding of the agency of the colonised by networking the pathos experiences of many colonised groups such as women and tribals as in methodological inclusivism, dalit theology creates an exclusive boundary around the pathos of the dalits, thus creating a double exclusion for itself as a developing ground for agency.

When advocacy has shown the potential to engage with agency methodological exclusivists are wary that advocacy could exhibit a false sense of solidarity. As exclusivists pressingly point out, agency is about living out and therefore solidarity could take the focus away from agency or instrumentalise the colonised.

An interesting factor that has strengthened the argument for agency is the theme of mystery. In the liberation theologies, mystery refers both to the Christian doctrinal sense of Trinity (Nirmal) and to the feminine divine (Dayam) to re-formulate Christian theology into theo/alogies for an inclusive vision of Dalit community. The presentation of mystery is from Christian traditions and beyond. Therefore, mystery offers multireligious resource to enhance the Christian understanding of Christology.

The presentation of mystery in the liberation theologies means a critique of the exclusive male Christology of the Christian tradition. It means a robust argument to see the divine mystery, the ultimate source of agency, present not just in the marginalised communities but also in the dominant traditions that offer advocacy to marginalised communities. While mystery exhibits the divine agency as a formidable front for the agency of the marginalised, it also moves beyond strictly exclusivist methodological boundaries.

Among the methodologies of liberation theologies, praxis has created spaces for for more open-ended conversations between the exclusive agency of the marginalised and the potential liberative resources of the advocates. From the discussion on spatial opportunism of Schmalz and the rightful recognition of the colonized as the majority among Indian Christians by Rajkumar, we observe that praxis demonstrates best the negotiable space between the colonised and the coloniser. However, the threat still is the movement towards the dominant model of Indian Christian theology where the culturally and politically dominant have the ability to take advantage of the negotiable space to colonise and recolonise. An important and critical observation to be made here is that despite being the majority in Indian Christian scenario, the exclusive agency of the marginalised could not bring about the liberation all by itself. It can be observed that, the Christian discourse of the colonised was caught up in a conundrum whether to claim its majority only within Christian context and seek its liberation or to gather interreligious resources, a macro approach, through inclusive discourses and movements to strengthen and speed up the liberative process.

The above explanations indicate that liberation theologies in India are largely confined to a historical understanding of colonisation and therefore use resistance and counter-response as their key hermeneutical position. The hermeneutics of counter-responses and resistance largely undermine the potential for a liberative engagement with those in solidarity who committedly strive to advance the agency of the colonised. But it is also to be noted that the liberation theologies have shown certain degrees of openness to engagement. But, there is also an unwritten line of priority that can be frequently observed in liberationist analysis in India: caste, class, gender, tribal/adivasis and ecological issues. The debates on the rights and agency of children need to usually wait for this cycle to complete.

Chapter 5

The Purposeful Triad
The Agency of the Child, the Rooted Solidarity of Adults and the Immanent Mystery of God and the Child

Introduction

The debates on the place and centrality of children in Christology and in liberationist theologies, including the child-focussed theologies, reinforce positive directions to advance the agency of the child. In contexts that are predominantly adult, the agency of the child must be duly complemented and supplemented by a robust understanding of rooted solidarity of the adults along with a robust theology of the immanent mystery of God. The understanding of the mystery of God and the mystery that surrounds the knowledge of child complement each other. Neither a clear understanding of the agency of the child nor a clear understanding of the responsible advocacy of the adults can be drawn from the child-focussed theologies so far. This chapter offers the triadic themes as fresh ways forward for an effective understanding of the agency of the child.

Marty's explanation of children as "mystery surrounded by mystery" offers a central argument that, if we have to envision a radically improved way of understanding children, then we need to have an equally radical shift from understand children as complex sets of problems to children as mystery. The idea of interaction with children should not constrained to the cultural "childness", something that one should grow out of, but to ascribe the divine characteristics to the child as frequently prescribed in the theology of Image of God. Marty wishes to take the line of thought that speaks of an "analogy of relation" where humans and God participate in each other's activities.[153] This analogy helps us offer enriched place both to the child and to God in our theological thought process. So, alongside the agency of the child are purposefully engaging hermeneutical partners: the rooted solidarity of adults and the immanent mysteries of God and of the child.

A detailed justification for the rooted-solidarity of the adults is more necessitated than ever before. Adults are contextually privileged because of legalities, cultural practices, politics and religious teachings that work in their favour. Even the most committed among the adults are endowed with adult-privileges. Even when legalities, theologies and cultural practices are reworked to accommodate and favour children, it is the adult community which is expected to take the lead in implementing these radical directives. Approaching the privilege of the adults positively, those adults in solidarity will be dedicatedly and critically able to comprehend the contextual nuances of the debates of adult-dominance and entitlements and their impacts on children's world. A new sociability emerging through such self-critical conversations among the adults suppose creating flexible yet committed configurations of agency and rooted-solidarity.

As regards the understanding of the mystery, while the children-related theologies in particular and Christian theological principles in general have indicated liberative eagerness and have strategically drawn liberative directions from the debates on the agency of the child from within Christian theology and from outside of it, they have not made robust headways to discuss the notion of divinity or mystery around the agency or centrality of children. This is with the fear that such a discourse would

---

[153] Marty, *The Mystery*, 66.

displace the understanding of the centrality of God or Jesus Christ to Christian faith, as discussed in chapter 3. By not being theologically proactive and imaginative to discuss the theme of mystery, the child-focussed theologies continue to perpetuate an adult-privileged discourse about God or Jesus because is the adults who interpret the powers associated with the mystery. With these challenges and promises, the following principles contribute towards opening up a deeper notion of the agency of the child, the rooted solidarity of the adults and an immanent understanding of the mystery.

Recreating Radical Conviviality

When the child-focussed theologies offer conceptual discussions with the framework of liberation theologies, it is anticipated to incorporate various liberative principles with a vision to create welcoming spaces. While the principal claim of the child-focussed theologies is to be liberative is in the right direction, the hermeneutical principles are not explored adequately. As observed in the debate on Christology and in the eclectic method takes the debate further by implying that praxis, a key hermeneutical proposition of liberation theology, could give an edge to the already present biblical-centred theories of children's development and care which are found wanting in Child Theologies. With this, Holistic Child Development suggests that restricted focus on biblical-centred theologies alone will restrict the scope of the theologies, and therefore praxis has to be consciously incorporated into the methodological discussion. The theological positions of Child theologies may well draw from these methodological explorations when they claim to promote the centrality of children.

The above debates have raised significant questions about various notions of agency that the child-focussed theologies have floated which concentrate more power in the adults in the interpretation of the agency of the child. The Child theologies exhibit attentiveness as well as a paternalistic tendency of trying to say that children have to be in the centre and then wanting the children to be silent or passive participants. However, the projected child continues to be passive or silent. The projection of the passive or silenced child as analogous to the child that Jesus placed in the midst of the disciples is a shrewd theological excess. In the light of the initial claim to re-present children in a positive light, such an interpretation is a regression from being advocates to being superior.

It can be observed that advancing the agency of the child, unlike the adult-agency, needs greater support of adults than in other liberationist streams. Even while agency co-exists alongside advocacy, the conceptual difficulties of the agency of the child have to be seen as compellingly different from and underprivileged than the adults who are responsible advocates. However, it also points to the fact that there is a sense of advocacy of the adults as agency that wishes to bring children to the centre of theological discourse. It is this advocacy that must open up more space to advance the agency of the child. In this challenging dialogical situation where the responsibility is on the adults to recognise the presence of children's agency, the advocates are called to see the domains of speechlessness of children.

Identifying Potential Creativity of Differences

Identifying the creative potentials of the differences is a positive driving forces for agency. In situations where differences are taken advantage of to recreate hierarchies, the objective of critiquing the unconstructive character of the differences is to neither recreate another hierarchy based on power differentials nor to eliminate marginal values that the differences project. Rather, the awareness of the differences leads to new transformations.

The child-focussed theologies constantly and imperceptibly reinforce the binary opposites of adult-child as methodological features while still claiming to advance the centrality of children. In the child-in-the-midst method, the adult intentions to prolong the adult-child binary is strongly underlined by projecting Christ as the power and source of the agency. By inference, questioning adult-dominance amounts to questioning adult-representations of Christ: the way the adults represent Christ and the adult depiction of Christ to favour the adult world. This is further indirectly reinforced by the adult-claims that the presence of passive children is adequate enough to discuss children's centrality. In the child-focussed theologies, the deeper intentions have been to bridge the differences between the understanding of the centrality of children and the patronising voices of adults. However, the child-focussed theologies predominantly exhibit patronising attitudes towards children.

The crucial idea that positive perception of differences brings about transformation emerges from the awareness of the differences itself.[154] However, the differences on the side of the disadvantaged children are interpreted as absence or lack. Further, unique differences that children project should not be relegated to the social margins nor should lead to the "silencing or elimination of minoritarian values" because these values are significant in identifying and exploring the agency of the colonized.[155]

The child-focussed theologies have deferred from exploring the positive notion of the conversation between the differentials. The adults have to engage with their dominant self to explore their potentials that harm advancing the agency of the child. The adults would as well discover their potential for rooted-solidarity to engage with children to discern their sense of responsibility in relation to children's needs and desires.

As observed in the challenges to Christology in chapter 3, children's views and the place of children in history offer us new insights in understanding the deeper shades to our views about Jesus Christ, that Jesus was a child himself and had gone through similar socio-cultural injustices that children of our times go through. Hence, Jesus is able to offer a new insight to our understanding of children as the signs to the Kingdom of God, thus enhancing the central place of the child. At the same time, the lens of the child helps us see how Jesus, as an adult, was socially and culturally conditioned too.

Agency as Seeking Belonging

Belonging and engaging in a new sociability gives power to the voiceless. The child-focussed theologies offer preliminary leads to discuss the sense of belonging and engaging. They seem to promote

---

[154] Bignall, *Postcolonial Agency*, 8.

[155] Bignall, *Postcolonial Agency*, 39.

the centrality of children in a world of new openness albeit in a limited manner. To bring it closer to Indian theological context, liberation theologies in India and Children-related theologies offer different understandings of desires to re-vision the idea of belonging positively. In the traditional liberation theologies, the dominant and the projected marginalized are all adults and therefore the nature of their desire to belong is different from desires of the marginalized children. Again, among children, it should be further stated that the desire exhibits differently among different age-groups of children.

Even in liberation theologies such as dalit, feminist, womanist, tribal and similar theologies, the marginalized among them could be empowered and made aware of their loss of agency perhaps more easily than with children. In these theologies, the names, faces and first-hand narratives of children are omitted although they belong to these castes, tribes and gender categories. While it could be argued that children between the age group of 10-18 make an impact on the policy decisions through gut-wrenching narratives of the violation of their rights and loss of dignity, the children among the lesser age group would not have even realised the loss of their power or the overpowering dominance of adults in the adult domain. Effectively, the children are not seen to belong to the ongoing and routine narratives of our societies.

Likewise, in the child-focussed theologies, it is not to completely reject the role of adults to attempt to bring the child to the centre of theological discussions. But it is to critique the inclusion and dominance of the narratives that disregard children, their contexts and their views. An over-emphasis of the theological configurations so far would invariably lead to reinstating modernity traits. In this light a practical understanding of the mystery gives children the power that the advocates have to recognise. Therefore I argue that the mystery is a strong factor in explaining the agency of the child alongside the deep solidarity of the adults. Multiple factors such as the agency, the rooted solidarity and the immanent mystery significantly resist the potential privileging of any one factor.

Mystery as an Interlocutor

The understanding of mystery is not restricted to the unexplainable ideas about God or Christ, or the unachievable acts by humans. The achievable and liveable example of the mystery is manifested in Jesus the Christ. Two prominent perspectives on mystery in ontological terms must be drawn from the works of Mark Lewis Taylor[156] and Martin Marty.[157] Taylor speaks of the "region of mystery" in relationship to subaltern discourse that offers leads for debates on the issues of children too. Taylor insists that any creation of the insignificant other must be revisited as a fertile region to grasp "this worldly mystery" for a deeper understanding of the 'other'. Translating Taylor's idea to the issues of children, the so-understood insignificant children can open up a world of wisdom, not of the world outside the realm of adult-dominant wisdom, but of children emerging from within our very own contexts. Likewise, Marty clarifies the aspects of God and Christ which underscore and support child advocacy, the agency of the child, and the ways God is already moving in the lives of children. Marty's exposition of eventful mystery invests positive power in children which provides potential insights to the agency of the child. The complexity of the issue of children and mystery should not be treated as a problem but more positively as an unexplored sense of mystery. The unexplored depths of mystery would facilitate the reduction of adult dominance rather than giving the adults more power.

A well clarified notion of mystery facilitates the adult-dominant world to be in rooted-solidarity with children while ascertaining that the adults do not turn to be colonising agents of children. This clarity is necessary because the notion of mystery in the child-focussed theology is instantly and uncritically related to God the Father and to Jesus Christ. Our traditional perceptions of God the Father and Jesus Christ have been criticized for dominant

---

[156] Mark Lewis Taylor, "Subalternity and Advocacy as Kairos for Theology," in *Opting for the Margins: Postmodernity and Liberation in Christian Theology,* ed. Joerg Rieger (Oxford: Oxford University Press, 2003): 40-41.

[157] Martin Marty, *The Mystery of the Child* (Grand Rapids/Cambridge: William B. Eerdmans Publishing Company, 2007), 52-53.

cultural and theological baggage they carry. Grobbelaar seems to have discerned the prevailing perception of God and Jesus Christ but have kept the explanations about them elusive. Grobbelaar recognizes that nature-nurture debate about childhood and children meet “in some mysterious ways” to create the structure of “grammar” for the ongoing discourse on children and theology.[158]

Taylor opens up the issue of mystery through his account of advocacy. Mystery is the differential that the engaging spaces offer especially to the advocating dominant. This mystery subsequently promotes responsible advocacy when the advocates potentially expose themselves to the context of solidarity and explore the liberative resources which is a movement away from their imperial self. The ability to accept the profound uncertainty in the face of the other enhances the value of mystery.

Marty's elucidation of mystery augments Taylor's thoughts on mystery. Mystery, for Marty, is “limitless contingencies, experiences, and choices...”[159] To extend this principle to understanding children, conceptualizing children demands an act of openness to see them beyond any one contingency such as their physicality or vulnerability. Their significance cannot be restricted just to the biblical notions of the gift of God, or as the source of covenant as promoted in the child-focussed theologies. Nor is it restricted to the mysterious silence of the child that could still show the way to the kingdom of God.

The Purposeful Triad: The Agency of the Child, the Rooted Solidarity of Adults and the Immanent Mystery of God and the Child

The theme of the agency of the child, along with the rooted- solidarity of adult-privileged communities and the the immanent mystery of God and the child constitute the factors for a qualitative agency of the child. The need for a configuration of themes is compelling and purposeful. Jayakiran Sebastian's call for interrelational and

---

[158] Jaan Grobbelaar and Gert Breed, *Theologies of Childhood and the Children of Africa* (Durbanville: AOSIS, 2016), 59.

[159] Marty, *Mystery*, 52-53.

reconciliatory hermeneutical movements resounds appropriately in the context of child-focussed theologies too. In the growing context of methodological exclusivism and exclusive agency within liberationist movement, Sebastian observes inter-relationship and interaction between dalit theology and other forms of theologizing, as well as between dalit and other communities, including those communities whose present status was achieved, at least in part, while not neglecting the use and abuse of dalit peoples.[160] It can be noticed that while agency of the colonised as a consequence of interrelationality is not entirely rejected, the core experiences of pathos is treated as significant and unique to understanding the agency of the marginalized.

The Agency of the Child

The understanding of the agency of the child as debated in the previous chapters includes the impact children make by their presence as social and political actors and also by their views and expressions. This agency is either the deliberate act or an unprompted communication that offers continued and enhanced ideas for change. The positive, creative and agentic presence of children can also be understood through received traditions such as religious scriptures and cultural practices that claim centrality of children. A robust understanding of agency is largely about the agency of the colonised children whose presence should keep stressing on new sociability. Explaining this contextually, the agency of the child also discloses itself in the situations of the violation of their rights where children start speaking up for their rights and dignity. The circumstances of speaking up for their rights is when children converse with adults or retaliate in predominantly adult-dominant contexts. Fierce conversations or retaliation has to be part of the definition of agency because children, by definition, fall within the age of 16, or sometimes even 18. Therefore, retaliation comes from a state of awareness of being wronged against. Therefore, the

---

[160] J. Jayakiran Sebastian, "Creative Exploration: Arvind P. Nirmal's Ongoing Contribution to Christian Theology," in *Bangalore Theological Forum,* XXXI/2 (December 1999): 48.

understanding of the agency of the child should consider different age groups and wide spectrum of awareness of children about their dignity. Age and awareness become important analytical factors. Understandably children of younger age and less aware of legalities of the society are unaware of their rights and dignity and therefore do not even realize the violation of their rights.

The Rooted Solidarity of the Adults

Much of the advancing of the agency of the child happen with rooted-solidarity as an adult responsibility. The theme 'rooted solidarity of the adults' constantly throws up some challenges. Initially, the dominant adult mindset has the moral challenge of identifying two conflicting areas: to create an affirmative space for the agency of the child and, simultaneously, time to create a space for its advocating act and solidarity without impinging on the potential space for the agency of the child.

Context-specific knowledge of the agency and the advocacy are foundational to the understanding of rooted solidarity. The openness to contextual knowledge of the adult-child binaries, their challenges and their potentials offer negotiable spaces for theory and praxis. As observed in liberation theologies in India and the child-focussed theologies in general, the advocates of the subalterns delicately, if not impeccably, recognise that grassroot activism at any scale is crucial as it challenges the notion of an established space. This is because the established spaces are rigid and less likely to grasp the availability of liberative resources outside their spaces. These explanations also open up spaces for a critique of the practice of advocacy or solidarity that adult-centric ideologies proclaim.

Advocacy is basically didactic in nature and its objective is to conscientize the public of discriminations and speak on behalf of the voiceless marginalized. The acts of conscientizing and speaking means good towards the agency of the marginalized, in our case, the child. The advocates are constantly challenged to journey through a transformative process between their entitled-self and their solidarity-self that represents the child, which finally upholds the agency of the child than the entitled adult-self. Failure in achieving this transformation leads to a failure in sincerely advancing the agency of the child.

Advocacy has the ability to misjudge the power to represent. When the subalterns speak the language of the dominant, the advocates must be able to discern it. Otherwise, it completes a vicious circle where the representers re-hear their own language in the expressions of the children to make it easier for them to represent, speak or preach their own perspective of the narrative. Advocacy may not be truthful to the oppressed narratives thus strangling the advancing of the agency of the marginalized.

Listening to and representing children in the context of advocacy has legal implications. In rights-violated situations, the advocates will have to resort to a legal language that is mostly couched in philosophical debates and probabilities rather than in the languages and emotions of children. The uniqueness of experiences may not find an authentic place in the legalese involving the violated-against children.

Joerg Rieger and Rosemarie Henkel-Rieger's explanation of 'deep solidarity' offers a noteworthy explanation and unpacks our thoughts for deeper questions on solidarity. For Rieger and Henkel-Rieger,

> "solidarity is no longer a matter of the relatively privileged trying to help the underprivileged and to solve their problems; rather, it is a matter of understanding that nothing will change unless we are addressing the problems of the world together. And deep solidarity is the recognition that we might be in the same boat."[161]

Crucial to Rieger and Henkel-Rieger's thoughts are moving beyond even the nuanced binaries of the relatively privileged-underprivileged. They explain their concept in the context of ruthless neoliberal capitalist economies where more people are getting underprivileged by the day only to see that all wealth and privileges are concentrated

---

[161] Rieger, J. & Henkel-Rieger, R., 'Deep Solidarity: Broadening the Basis of Transformation', HTS Teologiese Studies/Theological Studies 73(3), 2017, a4578. https://doi.org/10.4102/hts.v73i3.4578.

among a few. Rieger and Henkel-Rieger are mindful of the differences and "where all other forms of oppression along the lines of race, ethnicity, gender, sexuality, etc., are bundled."[162]

Expanding the scope of the boat metaphor in the context of adult-child binary, the existential journeys and travel of children and childhoods can happen at different levels of luxuries: the privileged in luxurious and secured means, while the underprivileged in the most unsafe boats to move across to cities, states and continents. When hit by the same storm or tempest on the same sea, the responses vary depending on degrees of security and privilege. The secured means have greater possibility of reaching the shores than the unsafe ones.

A deeper understanding of solidarity for the adult-centric world to exercise and to advance the agency of the child is 'rooted solidarity'. Rooted solidarity begins with the idea that adulthood has embodied of childhood experiences. The adults have their roots in their childhood. Their childhood would have experienced deprivation, biases and negligence as much as privileges and protection. For the agency of the child to be advanced, the adult community has to recall its own experiences and narratives of vulnerability and deprivation to empathize with children who face injustice and vulnerability. Rooted-Solidarity calls the adult world to empathetically listen to children and be responsibly descerning during the act of listening.

Empathetic and responsible listening further facilitates to engage and embody two narratives: the adults' own childhood narratives, and the stories and narrative of children which could be dissimilar to adults own narratives but coming from similar social and cultural contexts that belittle children, put children at risk and make children vulnerable. It is important for the adults to go back to our roots and see if we were once victimised or wronged against; what were some of the most vulnerable situations we have had been in? how have the memories of such victimisation conditioned our mindset to address the situations of victimization around us? Equally importantly as adults, when we are in the positions of power to make decisions or even in a position to influence the

162 Rieger, J. & Henkel-Rieger, R., 'Deep solidarity.

decisions, what do we become: perpetrators of violence or exhibit a sense of empathy to the victims? what mindset takes-over when we are in the position of power that will it be a selective amnesia that we were once victims and that it is our now time to enjoy the power and privilege that we were deprived of? Or, will it be a sense of deeply rooted solidarity in which we will not let recreate a sense of risk or vulnerability because we did not like to be at risk and vulnerable ourselves? The characteristics of rooted-solidarity involve a redefined responsibility of not just representing (as in advocacy) but also listening to an extent that finally what the adult world listens as individuals and groups will convert into a community activity of listening and opening up spaces for the voices of children. Such community activities will create flourishing spaces for more authentic agency of the child.

The Immanent Mystery

When adults explore deeper meanings of mystery in the differences that children offer, the adult communities heighten their sense of solidarity and responsibility than their dominance. This resonates with Taylor's explanation of the mysterious knowledge that is gained in a delirium caused through the unanswered questions in the engagement between the dominant and the vulnerable.

For the adults to see the presence of mystery in the presence and activities of children is a truly a liberating act. Listening to children is possible by seeing children as young persons and agents. The mystery of the agency of the child is an amalgam of the recognition that children are full persons and that listening to their views is as significant as listening to the adults in theological meaning-making. But one needs to be mindful of the challenging contextual paradox too. More often than not the agency of the child gets authenticated only when confirmed so by the adult world. To explain it from the view point of an adult advocate, the listening vocation of the adults is not the only time when the children would speak or verbalize their thoughts. But it is in the recognition of the children's desire to speak and in the readiness for a conversation about the unknown surrounding that engagement that one advances the agency of the child. Hence the liberative responsibility of the adult is to recognise that children have the capacity for agency because of their eventful mystery. Listening as a liberative activity fulfils the act of the rooted-solidarity and recognizes the mystery that is embodied in children. It is in the adults interacting actively with the child that advances the child's agency and sees the agency of the child beyond the restricted realm of the adult-child binary. The mystery challenges perpetuation of the binary and the colonisation. Mystery presents awe and wonder in the face of an interaction with children. When the adults willingly consent to the mystery in children, they open up to the potentials of children's agency.

Mystery is a robust factor in advancing the agency of the child. Mystery not only emphasizes the eventful presence and power of children in relation to the dominant adults; it also opens up to creative engagements in transforming the dominant adults towards rooted solidarity. Therefore, mystery holds the key for a continuous engagement between the agency of the child and the rooted solidarity of adults. The mystery here does not just connote the Divine, the God or Jesus Christ, but also many creative and unexplored ways of knowing, being and becoming the child.

Bibliography

Books

"Post-colonialism/Postcolonialism." In *Post-Colonial Studies: The Key Concepts*, edited by Bill Ashcroft, Gareth Griffiths and Helen Tiffin, 186-187. London and New York: Routledge, 2002.

Amirtham, Metti. *Women in India: Negotiating Body, Reclaiming Agency*. Delhi: ISPCK, 2011.

Appiah, Kwame Anthony. "Understanding 'Post' in *Postmodernism and Postcolonialism." In Contemporary Postcolonial Theory: A Reader*, edited by Padmini Mongia. London: Arnold, 1996.

Ayrookuzhiel, Abraham. "Distinctive Characteristics of Folk Traditions. A Proposal for the Study of the Religious Heritage of the Dalits: Some Methodological Considerations." In *Religions of the Marginalized: Towards a Phenomenology and the Methodology of Study*, edited by Gnana Robinson. Bangalore/ Delhi: UTC/ ISPCK, 1998.

Balagopalan, Sarada. *Inhabiting 'Childhood': Children, Labour and Schooling in Postcolonial India*. London: Palgrave Macmillan, 2014.

Bastiaan Wielenga, "Liberation Theology in Asia." In *The Cambridge Companion to Liberation Theology*: Second Edition, edited by Christopher Rowland. Cambridge University Press, 2007.

Bennett, Zoe. "'Action is the Life of All': The Praxis-based Epistemology of Liberation Theology." *The Cambridge Companion to Liberation Theology*. 2nd edition, edited by, Christopher Rowland. 39-54. Cambridge: Cambridge University Press, 2007.

Bhabha, Homi. *The Location of Culture*. Abingdon: Routledge, 1994.

Bignall, Simone. *Postcolonial Agency: Critique and Constructivism*. Edinburgh: Edinburgh University Press, 2010.

Boff, Leonardo. "Christ's Liberation via Oppression." *In Frontiers of Theology in Latin America*, edited by Roselin Gibellini. Maryknoll, New York: Orbis, 1979.

Brewster, Dan. "Themes and Implications of Holistic Child Development Programming in Seminaries." In *Children at Risk: Issues and Challenges,* edited by Jesudason Jeyaraj, 32-48. Bangalore: Christian Forum for Child Development/ISPCK, 2009.

Chowdhry, Geeta. "Postcolonial Interrogations of Child Labour." In *Power, Postcolonialism and International Relations: Reading Race, Gender and Class*, edited by Geeta Chowdhry and Sheila Nair, 1st Indian Reprint. London and New York: Routledge, 2003.

Clarke, Sathianathan. *Dalits and Christianity: Subaltern Religion and Liberation Theology in India*. New Delhi: Oxford University Press, 1999.

__________________. "Dalit Theology." In *Dictionary of Third World Theologies*, edited by Virginia Fabella and R. S. Sugirtharajah, 64-65. Maryknoll, New York: Orbis Books, 2000.

__________________. "Dalit Theology: An Introductory and Interpretative Theological Exposition." In *Dalit Theology in the Twenty-first Century: Discordant Theological Voices, Discerning Pathways,* edited by Sathianathan Clarke, Deenabandhu Manchala and Philip Vinod Peacock, 19-37. New Delhi: Oxford University Press, 2010.

Collier, John. "Preface." In *Toddling to the Kingdom: Child Theology at Work in the Church*, edited by John Collier, 7-10. London: Child Theology Movement, 2009.

Coorilos, Geevarghese Mor. "Foreword." *Revisiting the Other: Discourses on Postmodern Theology*. Vinayaraj Y. T. Tiruvalla: Christava Sahitya Samithi, 2010.

Davidson, Donald. "Agency." In *Essays on Actions and Events*, 3-19. Oxford: Oxford University Press, 1980.

Dayam, Joseph Prabhakar. "Gonthemma Korika: Reimagining the Divine Feminine in Dalit Theology." In *Dalit Theology in the Twenty-first Century: Discordant Theological Voices, Discerning Pathways,* edited by Sathianathan Clarke, Deenabandhu Manchala and Philip Vinod Peacock, 137-149. New Delhi: Oxford University Press, 2010.

Dietrich, Gabriele. *A New Thing on Earth: Hopes and Fears Facing Feminist Theology,* Delhi/ Madurai: ISPCK/ TTS, 2001.

Gandhi, Leela. *Postcolonial Theory: A Critical Introduction.* New York: Colombia University Press, 1998.

Gideon, Rohan. "The Challenges of Subjectivity of Children to Christology", Bangalore Theological Forum, Vol. LI, No. 2 (Dec. 2019): 168-180.

_____________. "Children's Agency and Edinburgh 2010: The Great Commission or a Greater Omission?" in Mitzi Smith and Jayachitra Lalitha eds. *Teaching All Nations: Interrogating the Matthean Great Commission*, Minneapolis: Fortress Press, 2014: 195-216.

_____________. "Child Theology and Liberation Theologies: Their Convergence and its Implications" in Jesudason et. al. eds. *Repairers of Broken Walls: Essays on Holistic Child Development*, Bangalore: CFCD-India, 2014: 188-199.

_____________. *Child Labour in India: Its Challenges for Theological Thought and Christian Ministry in India*, Delhi/Nagpur: ISPCK/ NCCI, 2011.

_____________. "Soteriology and Children's Vulnerabilities and Agency" in Marcia J. Bunge ed. Child Theology: Diverse Methods and Global Perspectives, Maryknoll: Orbis Books, 2021: 90-107.

Grey, Mary. "Feminist Theology: A Critical Theology of Liberation." In *The Cambridge Companion to Liberation Theology*: Second Edition, edited by Christopher Rowland. 105-122. Cambridge University Press, 2007.

Grobbelaar, Jan. *Child Theology and the African Context*. London: Child Theology Movement Ltd: 2012.

Illaiah, Kancha. *Why I am not a Hindu: A Sudra Critique of Hindu Philosophy, Culture and Political Economy*. Calcutta: Samya, 2005.

Jayachitra, Lalitha. "Jesus and Ambedkar: Exploring Common Loci for Dalit Theology and Dalit Movements." In *Dalit Theology in the Twenty-first Century: Discordant Theological Voices, Discerning Pathways,* edited by Sathianathan Clarke, Deenabandhu Manchala and Philip Vinod Peacock, 121-136. New Delhi: Oxford University Press, 2010.

Jayakumar, Samuel. *Dalit Consciousness and Christian Conversion: Historical Resources for a Contemporary Debate*. Oxford/Delhi: Regnum International/ISPCK, 1999.

Jensen, David H. *Graced Vulnerability: A Theology of Childhood.* Cleveland: Pilgrim, 2005.

Jeremiah, Anderson H. M. *Community and Worldview Among Paraiyars of South India: 'Lived' Religion*. London: Bloosmbury Academic, 2013.

Jeremiah, Anderson H. M. "Exploring New Facets of Dalit Christology: Critical Interaction with J. D. Crossan's Portrayal of Historical Jesus." In *Dalit Theology in the Twenty- first Century: Discordant Theological Voices, Discerning Pathways,* edited by Sathianathan Clarke, Deenabandhu Manchala and Philip Vinod Peacock, 150-167. New Delhi: Oxford University Press, 2010.

Jeyaraj, Jesudason B. "Child in the Midst: Incarnation and Child Theology." In *Children at Risk: Issues and Challenges,* edited by Jesudason Jeyaraj, 49-72. Bangalore: Christian Forum for Child Development/ISPCK, 2009.

Larbeer, Mohan P. *Ambedkar on Religion: A Liberative Perspective*. Madurai /Delhi: DRC/ISPCK, 2003.

Longchar, A. Wati, ed. *An Exploration of Tribal Theology*. Jorhat: Tribal Study Centre, ETC, 1997.

Longchar, A. Wati. *An Emerging Asian Theology: Tribal Theology, Issue, Method and Perspectives*. Jorhat: Tribal Study Centre, ETC, 2000.

Lott, Eric. *Religious Faith, Human Identity: Dangerous Dynamics in Global and Indian Life*. Bangalore: Asian Trading Corporation & United Theological College, 2005.

Lott, Eric. *Religious Faith, Human Identity: Dangerous Dynamics in Global and Indian Life*. Bangalore: Asian Trading Corporation & United Theological College, 2005.

Lott, Eric. *Religious Faith, Human Identity: Dangerous Dynamics in Global and Indian Life*. Bangalore: Asian Trading Corporation & United Theological College, 2005.

Marty, Martin. *The Mystery of the Child.* Grand Rapids/Cambridge: William B. Eerdmans Publishing Company, 2007.

Massey, James and T. K. John SJ. "Concept Paper: Centre for Dalit/ Subaltern Studies." In *Frontiers in Dalit Hermeneutics.* Edited by James Massey, and Samson Prabhakar. Bangalore/Delhi: BTESSC/ SATHRI & CDSS, 2005.

Massey, James. *Dalits in India: Religion as a Source of Bondage or Liberation with Special Reference to Christians.* New Delhi: Manohar Publishers and Distributors, 1995.

__________. *Down Trodden: The Struggle of India's Dalits for Identity, Solidarity and Liberation.* Geneva: WCC, 1997.

Melanchthon, Monica Jyotsna. "Akkamahadevi and the Samaritan Woman: Paradigms of Resistance and Spirituality." In *Border Crossings: Cross-Cultural Hermeneutics,* edited by D. N. Premnath. Maryknoll, Orbis Books, 2007.

__________. "The Servant in the Book of Judith: Interpreting her Silence, Telling her Story." In *Dalit Theology in the Twenty- first Century: Discordant Theological Voices, Discerning Pathways,* edited by Sathianathan Clarke, Deenabandhu Manchala and Philip Vinod Peacock, 231-241. New Delhi: Oxford University Press, 2010.

__________. "Bathsheba Reconsidered: Sexual Violation and After." In *Gender, Religion und Kultur, Theologischen Akzente, Band 6.* Edited by Renata Jost. Stuttgart: Kohlhammer Verlag, 2010: 77-100.

__________. "Dalit Readers of the Word: The Quest for Hermeneutics and Method." In *Frontiers in Dalit Hermeneutics*, edited by James Massey and Samson Prabhakar. Bangalore/Delhi: BTESSC-SATHRI/CDSS, 2005.

Minz, Nirmal. "The Study of Tribal Religion in India." In *Re-visioning India's Religious Traditions*, edited by David C. Scott and Israel Selvanayagam. Delhi/Bangalore: ISPCK/UTC, 1996.

__________. *Rise Up, My People, and Claim the Promise. The Gospel Among the Tribes of India*. Delhi: ISPCK, 1997.

Mohanty, Manoranjan. Class, Caste and Gender, 3rd reprint. New Delhi, SAGE, 2006.

Mongia, Padmini, ed. *Contemporary Postcolonial Theory: A Reader.* London: Arnold, 1996.

Moore-Gilbert, Bart. *Postcolonial Theory: Contexts, Practices, Politics.* London: Verso, 1997.

Mor Coorilose, Geevarghese. "Dalit Theology and its Future Course." In *Dalit Theology in the Twenty-first Century: Discordant Theological Voices, Discerning Pathways,* edited by Sathianathan Clarke, Deenabandhu Manchala and Philip Vinod Peacock, 168-177. New Delhi: Oxford University Press, 2010.

Nalunnakkal, George Mathew. *Green Liberation: Towards an Integral Ecotheology*. Delhi: IPSCK/NCCI, 1999.

Nambissan, Geetha B. "Social Exclusion, Children's Work and Education." In *Child Labour and the Right to Education in South Asia: Needs versus Rights*, edited by Naila Kabeer, Geetha B. Nambissan and Ramya Subramanian. New Delhi: Sage Publications, 2003.

Nirmal, Arvind P. "A Diaologue with Dalit Literature." In *Towards a Dalit Theology*. edited by M. E. Prabhakar. New Delhi: ISPCK, 1988.

__________. "A Dialogue with Dalit Literature." In *Towards A Dalit Theology*, edited by M. E. Prabhakar. Delhi: ISPCK, 1988.

__________. and V. Devasahayam, eds. *Dr. B.R. Ambedkar: A Centenary Tribute*. Madras: Gurukul, 1991.

__________. "A Diaologue with Dalit Literature." In *Towards a Dalit Theology,* edited by M. E. Prabhakar. New Delhi: ISPCK, 1988.

__________. "Towards a Christian Dalit Theology." In *Heuristic Explorations.* Madras: CLS, 1990.

Olga Niewenhuys, "The Paradox of Child Labour and Anthropology," *The Oxford India Companion to Sociology and Anthropology*, edited by Veena Das (New Delhi: Oxford University Press, 2003), 940-941.

Omvedt, Gail. *Caste, Land and Politics in Indian States.* New Delhi: Authors Guild Publication, 1982.

__________. *Dalit Visions: The Anti- caste Movement and the Constitution of an Indian Identity.* Hyderabad: Orient Longman, 2006.

Privett, Peter. "Prologue: The Thirtieth Anniversary of the International Year of the Child." In *Through the Eyes of the Child: New Insights in Theology from a Child's Perspective,* edited by Anne Richards and Peter Privet, xv-xx. London: Church House Publishing, 2009.

Pui- Lan, Kwok, Don H. Compier, and Joerg Riegers, eds. *Empire and the Christian Tradition: New Readings of Classical Theologians.* Minneapolis: Fortress Press, 2007.

Rajkumar, Peniel. "The Diversity and Dialectics of Dalit Dissent and Implications." In *Dalit Theology in the Twenty-first Century: Discordant Theological Voices, Discerning Pathways,* edited by Sathianathan Clarke, Deenabandhu Manchala and Philip Vinod Peacock, 55-76. New Delhi: Oxford University Press, 2010.

__________. *Dalit Theology and Dalit Liberation: Problems, Paradigms and Dalit Liberation.* Surrey: Ashgate, 2010.

Said, Edward W. *Reflections on Exile and Other Literary and Cultural Essays.* London: Grants Books, 2001.

Shah, Ghanshyam, ed. *Dalit Identity Politics: Cultural Subordination and the Dalit Challenge,* Vol. 2. New Delhi/London: Sage Publications/Thousand Oaks: 2001.

Shier-Jones, Angela, ed. *Children of God: Towards a Theology of Childhood*. Peterborough, UK: Epworth, 2007.

Spivak, Gayatri Chakravarti. In Other Worlds: Essays in Cultural Politics. New York/London: Routledge, 1988.

Sugirtharajah, R. S. "Postcolonial Biblical Interpretation." In *Voices from the Margin*, Revised and Expanded Third Edition, edited by R. S. Sugirtharajah. Maryknoll: Orbis Book, 2006.

__________. *Exploring Postcolonial Biblical Criticism: History, Method, Practice*. Chichester: Wiley-Blackwell, 2012.

__________. *Postcolonial Reconfigurations*, London: SCM Press, 2003.

Syiemlieh, B. J. "Contextual Interpretation of the New Testament in Northeast India: A Search for Principles and Methods." In *Tribal Theology and the Bible: A Search for Contextual Relevance*, edited by Yangkahao Yashum. Rajabai, Jorhat: Tribal Study Centre/Eastern Theological College, 2011.

Taylor, Mark Lewis. 'Subalternity and Advocacy as Kairos for Theology.' In *Opting for the Margins: Postmodernity and Liberation in Christian Theology*, edited by Joerg Rieger, http://oxfordindex.oup.com/view/10.1093/019516119X.003.0002.

Vinayaraj, Y. T., "Envisioning a Postmodern Method of doing Dalit Theology." In *Dalit Theology in the Twenty- first Century: Discordant Theological Voices, Discerning Pathways,* edited by Sathianathan Clarke, Deenabandhu Manchala and Philip Vinod Peacock, 93-103. New Delhi: Oxford University Press, 2010.

Wall, John. *Ethics in Light of Childhood*. Washington: Georgetown University Press, 2010.

White, Keith and Haddon Willmer. "Our Response" In *Toddling to the Kingdom: Child Theology at Work in the Church*, edited by John Collier London: Child Theology Movement, 2009.

White, Keith. "The Child in the Midst of the Biblical Witness." In *Toddling to the Kingdom: Child Theology at Work in the Church*, edited by John Collier, 154-160. London: Child Theology Movement, 2009.

__________. "'Come Over to Macedonia and Help us': Reflections on Child Theology and Holistic Child Development." In *Repairers of Broken Walls: Essays on Holisitic Child Development,* edited by J. B. Jeyaraj et. al. Bangalore: CFCD-India, 2014.

__________. "Child Theology, Loder, and Holistic Child Development (HCD)." In *The Logic of the Spirit in Human Thought and Experience: Exploring the Vision of James E. Loder Jr.* edited by Dana R. Wright and Keith White. Oregon: Pickwick, 2014.

Journals

Ahearn, Laura M. "Agency." Journal of Linguistic Anthropology, Vol. 9, Nos. 1-2 (1999): 12-15.

Ahmed, Aijaz. "The Politics of Literary Postcoloniality." Race and Class. Vol. 36, No. 3 (1995): 1-20.

Aleaz, K. P. "A Tribal Theology from a Tribal World-View." *Indian Journal of Theology* Vol. 44, No. 1 & 2 (2002): 20-30.

Arul Raja, Maria. "Living through Conflicts: The Spirit of Subaltern Resurgence." *Vidya Jothi Theological Review*, Vol. 65 (June 2001): 465-476.

__________. "Perspectives of Dalit Hermeneutics." *Gurukul Journal of Theological Studies* Vol. XVI, Nos. 1&2 (Jan. and July, 2005): 25-30.

Azadi India Foundation, Child Labour in India, http://azadindia.org/social-issues/child-labour-in-india.html (August 2007).

Basu, Kaushik. http://www.essex.ac.uk/armedcon/story_id/000413.pdf (9. 11. 2007).

Bhakiaraj, Paul Joshua. "From Invisibility to Indispensability: Sketches for an Indian Child Theology." *Dharma Deepika* 28/12/2 (July-December, 2008): 54-67.

Bignall, Simone. "Deleuze and Foucault on Desire and Power." *Angelaki* 13/1 (2008): 127-149.

Bunge, Marcia J. "Theologies of Childhood and Child theologies: International Initiatives to Deepen Reflection on Children and

Childhood in the Academy and Religious Communities." *Dharma Deepika* 28/12/2 (July-December, 2008): 33-53.

__________. "The Child, Religion, and the Academy: Developing Robust Theological and Religious Understandings of Children and Childhood", The Journal of Religion, Vol. 86, No. 4 (October 2006): 549-579.

Caldwell, Raymond. "Agency and Change: Re-evaluating Foucault's Legacy." *Organization* Vol. 14, No. 6: 2 (2007): 1-24.

Clarke, Sathianathan: "Viewing the Bible through the Eyes and Ears of Subalterns in India," *Biblical Interpretation.* Vol. 10, No. 3 (2002): 245-266.

__________. "The Jesus of Nineteenth Century Indian Christian Theology." *Studies in World Christianity* Vol. 5, No. 1: 32-46.

__________. "Viewing the Bible through the Eyes and Ears of Subalterns in India." http://www.religion-online.org/showarticle.asp?title=2444 (20th Dec. 2012).

Dietrich, Gabriele. "Why Should Postcolonial Feminist Theology Need to Relate to People's Movements?", *Asian Journal of Theology* Vol. 19, No. 1 (April 2005): 166-187.

Dillen, Annemie. "Children Between Liberation and Care: Ethical Perspectives on the Rights of Children and Parent–child Relationships." *International Journal of Children's Spirituality.* Vol. 11, No. 2, August 2006, pp. 237-250.

Estep, James Riley, Jr. "Childhood Transformation: Toward an Educational Theology of Childhood Conversion & Spiritual Formation." *Stone-Campbell Journal.* Vol. 5, No. 2 Fall (2002): 183-206.

Core Values of Global Alliance of Holistic Child Development: http://www.HolisticChildDevelopment-alliance.org/intro/aboutus (accessed June 2013).

Gideon, Rohan. "'Child-In-The-Midst' Method and Contemporary Children-Related Theologies: A Critical Survey." Bangalore Theological Forum, XLVIII/1: 61-73.

____________ . "Migration and Refugee Children: Revisiting the Theology of Incarnation," Theology, 120/5 (September/October

2017):http://www.HolisticChildDevelopment-alliance.org/intro/aboutus.

Ives, Peter. "Language, Agency and Hegemony." *Critical Review of International Social and Political Philosophy,* 8/4 (December, 2005): 455-468.

Jeyakumar. "Children as Impressions of God's Reign." *Iraiyiyal Malar* 1990: 9-10.

Lachman, Kathryn. "The Allure of Counterpoint: History and Reconciliation in the Writing of Edward Said and Assia Djebar." *Research in African literatures* Vol. 41, No. 4 (Winter 2010): 162-186.

Louai, El Habib. "Retracing the Concept of the Subaltern from Gramsci to Spivak: Historical Developments and New Applications." *African Journal of History and Culture (AJHC)* Vol. 4, No. 1 (January 2012): 4-8.

Louis, Prakash. "Editorial," Social Action Vol. 54, No. 4 (Oct-Dec), iv-v.

Melanchthon, Monica Jyotsna. "Dalits, Bible, and Method." http://sblsite.org/Article.aspx?ArticleID=459.

Nalunnakkal, George Mathew. Towards an Organic Womanism: http://www.elca.org/What-We-Believe/Social-Issues/Journal-of-Lutheran-Ethics/Issues/December-2003/Towards-an-Organic-Womanism-New-Contours-of-Ecofeminism-in-India.aspx (23.5.2012).

National Council of Churches Review Vol. CXXVII, No. 7 (Aug. 2007).

Nkurunziza, Deusdedit R. K. "African Theology of Childhood in Relation to Child Labour." *African Ecclesial Review*, Vol. 46, No. 2 (2004): 121-138.

Oommen, George. "The Emerging Dalit Theology: A Historical Appraisal." *Indian Church History Review*, Vol. XXXIV, No. 1 (June 2000): 19-37.

Racevskis, Karlis. "Edward Said and Michel Foucault: Affinities and Dissonances." *Research in African Literatures*, Vol. 36, No. 3 (Autumn, 2005): 83-97.

Raman, Vasanthi. *Globalisation and Child Labour,* http://www.revolutionarydemocracy.org/rdv4n1/childlab.htm (Children's Day, 2007).

Roy Chowdhury, Supriya. "Globalization and Labour." *Economic and Political Weekly* Vol. 39, No. 4 (Jan. 3 2004), 105.

Rufus, Penieel [sic] Jesudason. "The Problem of 'Methodological Fidelity' in Identify-Specific Hermeneutics and the Pertinence of 'Ethological' Hermeneutics." *Bangalore Theological Forum* Vol. XXXVIII, No. I (June 2006): 120-144.

Sarkar, Siddhartha. "Theorizing in Informal Sector: Concept and Context." *Social Action* Vol. 54, No. 4 (Oct.-Dec. 2004): 359-373.

Schmalz, Mathew N. "Dalit Catholic Tactics of Marginality at a North Indian Mission." *History of Religions*, Vol. 44, No. 3 (February 2005): 216-251.

Sebastian, J. Jayakiran. "'Can We Now Bypass that Truth?' Interrogating the Methodology of Dalit Theology." *Transformation* Vol. 25, Nos. 2 & 3 (April & July 2008): 80-91.

Sebastian, J. Jayakiran. "Creative Exploration: Arvind P. Nirmal's Ongoing Contribution to Christian Theology." *Bangalore Theological Forum*, Vol. XXXI, No. 2 (December 1999): 44-52.

Shiri, Godwin. "Study of Religion: Ayrookuzhiel's Search for a New Approach in the Context of Dalit Theology." *Religion and Society*, Vol. 43, No. 3 (September 1998): 39-53.

Singh, Avtar. "Child Labour Problems and Prospects: Socio-Legal Measures." *Social Action* Vol. 54, No. 4 (Oct.-Dec.), 396-97.

Sinha, Shantha. "Child Labour and Education." *Seminar* 474 (February 1994), 14-15.

Spivak, Gayatri Chakravorty interview by Leon de Kock, "New Nation Writers Conference in South Africa." *Ariel: A Review of International English Literature* Vol. 23, No. 3 (1992): 29-47.

Thatcher, Adrian. "Theology and Children: Towards a Theology of Childhood." *Transformation: An International Journal of Holistic Mission* Vol. 23, No. 194 (2006): 194-199.

__________. "A Theology of Liberation for Children." http://www.adrianthatcher.org/data/resources/a%20theology%20of%20liberation%20for%20children.pdf.

UNICEF, India-Child Labour, http://www.unicef.org/infobycountry/india_statistics.html1 (14 Novemeber, 2007).

Verma, Amit. "Why Child Labour?" http://www.org/rdv4n1/childlab.htm (November 14, 2007).

Wall, John. "Children and Political Representation: The Challenge of the Gift", *Journal of Childhood and Religion*, Vol. 1, No. 5 (July 2010): 1-32.

Interviews

Israel Selvanayagam. Chennai, India.

J. B. Jeyaraj. Madurai, India.

Siga Arles. Bangalore, India.

Email Correspondences

E-mail to the author on June 1, 2013: Sunny Tan

E-mail to the author on August, 2013: Keith White